The Android AI Developer's Guide

Generative Models and On-Device Implementation

By Carlos Smith

Table of Contents

Introduction

Chapter 1: Android AI Fundamentals

Chapter 2: Setting Up Your AI Development Environment

Chapter 5: Natural Language Processing (NLP) on Android

- 5.1 Text Classification and Sentiment Analysis
- 5.2 On-Device Language Models and Text Generation
- 5.3 Speech Recognition and Text-to-Speech Integration

Chapter 6: Generative AI with the Gemini API

- 6.1 Introduction to Gemini Models and API
- 6.2 Text and Image Generation with Gemini
- 6.3 Prompt Engineering and Creative Applications
- 6.4 Google AI Studio workflow

Chapter 7: Building Multimodal AI Applications

- 7.1 Combining Text and Image Generation
- 7.2 Interactive and Context-Aware AI Experiences
- 7.3 Practical Multimodal App Development Examples

Chapter 8: Fine-Tuning and Model Adaptation

- 8.1 Transfer Learning for Android AI
- 8.2 Adapting Pre-trained Models for Specific Tasks
- 8.3 Performance Optimization and Customization

Chapter 9: Deployment and Performance Optimization

Introduction

Welcome to a journey into the exciting world of Artificial Intelligence on Android. If you're like me, you've probably been fascinated by the rapid advancements in AI, especially in the realm of generative models and on-device machine learning. And if you're holding this book, you're ready to take that fascination and turn it into real, tangible skills. You're ready to build the future.

Why Android AI Matters

Let's start with a simple question: why Android? Well, for starters, it's everywhere. Billions of devices, a vast ecosystem, and a thriving community. That means the potential impact of AI on Android is immense. We're not just talking about cool demos; we're talking about real-world applications that can improve lives, enhance creativity, and revolutionize how we interact with technology.

Think about it. On-device AI can personalize experiences without sacrificing privacy. Imagine a camera app that instantly generates artistic filters based on your surroundings, or a language learning app that adapts to your speech patterns in real-time. These are just glimpses of what's possible when we bring powerful AI directly to the user's device.

And then there's the cloud. Generative models like Gemini, when paired with the cloud, open up entirely new possibilities. Creating realistic images from text prompts, generating engaging stories, or even building interactive AI assistants. The combination of on-device and cloud-based AI is where the magic truly happens.

Generative Models & On-Device ML: An Overview

Now, let's break down the core concepts we'll be exploring in this book.

- **Generative Models:** These are the creative engines of AI. They learn the underlying patterns in data and then generate new, original content. Think of them as artists who can create images, write stories, or compose music. We'll be focusing on how to leverage models like Gemini to bring these creative capabilities to your Android apps.
- **On-Device Machine Learning:** This is all about running AI models directly on the user's device. It's about speed, privacy, and reliability. By processing data

locally, we can build apps that are responsive and secure. We'll be diving deep into TensorFlow Lite and MediaPipe, the tools that make on-device ML a reality.

Why combine them? Because together, they offer the best of both worlds. On-device ML handles real-time, privacy-sensitive tasks, while cloud-based generative models bring the heavy-lifting creative power.

A Personal Note: When I first started exploring on-device ML, I was blown away by the possibilities. Running a complex object detection model on my phone felt like magic. And then, when I began experimenting with generative models, I realized we're on the cusp of a new era of interactive and creative applications. I'm excited to share that journey with you.

Book Roadmap

This book is structured to guide you from the fundamentals to advanced techniques. We'll start by setting up your development environment and understanding the core concepts of on-device ML. Then, we'll dive into practical applications, building real-world examples with TensorFlow Lite and MediaPipe.

Next, we'll explore the power of generative models with the Gemini API, learning how to create multimodal applications and fine-tune models for specific tasks. We'll also cover essential topics like performance optimization, deployment, and responsible AI development.

Here's a quick overview of what you can expect:

- **Chapters 1-3:** We'll build a solid foundation, understanding the basics of Android AI development.
- **Chapters 4-5:** You'll learn to implement practical on-device ML with Computer Vision and NLP.
- **Chapters 6-7:** We will explore the Gemini API and how to create generative AI applications.
- **Chapters 8-10:** You'll learn advanced techniques and best practices for creating powerful, efficient, and ethical AI apps.
- **Chapter 11:** We'll look ahead to the future of Android AI.

This book is designed to be hands-on. You'll find plenty of code examples, practical tips, and real-world projects to help you solidify your understanding.

So, let's get started. By the end of this book, you'll have the skills and knowledge to build amazing AI-powered Android apps. Let's create something extraordinary

Chapter 1: Android AI Fundamentals

Before we jump into the exciting world of coding AI into our Android apps, it's crucial to lay a solid foundation. Think of this chapter as our "AI for Android 101" course. We'll cover the core concepts, discuss the trade-offs, and touch upon the ethical side of things. Let's get started!

1.1 Core Concepts of Machine Learning for Android

Let's get down to the brass tacks of machine learning (ML) as it applies to Android development. You've probably heard the buzzwords, but what does it *actually* mean when we want to put ML into our apps? Let's demystify it.

The Foundation: Learning from Data

At its heart, ML is about teaching computers to learn patterns from data. Instead of explicitly programming every rule, we feed the machine examples, and it figures out the underlying relationships. This is crucial for Android because it allows us to build apps that adapt and improve over time, based on user interactions and data.

Key ML Paradigms

When we talk about ML on Android, we're primarily dealing with a few key paradigms:

- **Supervised Learning:**
  - This is the workhorse. We provide the model with labeled data—meaning, data with "answers." Think of it as training a dog with treats and commands. For example, we might show the model thousands of images of cats and dogs, labeled accordingly.
  - **Why it's vital for Android:** Image recognition, object detection, and sentiment analysis all fall under this category. Imagine an app that can recognize different types of plants from photos or analyze user reviews to understand sentiment.
  - **My take:** Supervised learning feels like teaching a student with a textbook and answer key. You guide the learning process, and the model gradually gets better at predicting outcomes.

- **Unsupervised Learning:**
  - Here, we give the model unlabeled data and let it find hidden patterns. Think of it as exploring a new city without a map.
  - **Why it's vital for Android:** Clustering users based on behavior, detecting anomalies in sensor data, and grouping similar images.
  - **My take:** Unsupervised learning is like letting a detective loose on a crime scene. The detective has to piece together the clues without knowing the answer beforehand.
- **Reinforcement Learning:**
  - The model learns by interacting with an environment and receiving rewards or penalties. Think of it as training a robot to navigate a maze.
  - **Why it's vital for Android:** While less common in typical Android apps, it's relevant for things like optimizing user interfaces or creating adaptive game AI.
  - **My take:** Reinforcement learning is like teaching a child through trial and error. The child learns

what works and what doesn't, based on the consequences of their actions.

Android's ML Landscape

For Android developers, a few core concepts are crucial:

- **Models:** The learned representation of the data. They're the "brains" of our AI apps.
- **Training:** The process of creating a model from data. This often happens in the cloud, but on device training is a growing area.
- **Inference:** The process of using a trained model to make predictions on new data. This is where Android shines, running models on-device for real-time interactions.
- **Tensors:** Multi-dimensional arrays, the fundamental data structure in TensorFlow Lite. Understanding tensors is essential for working with ML models on Android.

Practical Considerations

When bringing ML to Android, we must keep device limitations in mind.

- Mobile devices have less processing power and memory than cloud servers.
- We need to optimize models for on-device performance.
- We must consider user privacy and data security.

Why This Matters

Understanding these core concepts is the foundation for building intelligent Android apps. It allows us to create experiences that are personalized, adaptive, and engaging.

1.2 On-Device vs. Cloud-Based AI: Trade-offs

When it comes to integrating AI into our Android apps, one of the first and most important decisions we need to make is where to run our models. Do we keep them on the user's device, or do we send data to the cloud for processing? Let's break down the pros and cons of each approach.

On-Device AI: Power in Your Pocket

On-device AI, as the name suggests, runs machine learning models directly on the user's device. This offers several key advantages:

- **Privacy:**

- Data stays on the device, reducing the risk of sensitive information being exposed.
- This is crucial for apps that handle personal data.

- **Latency:**
  - Inference is performed locally, resulting in faster response times.
  - This is essential for real-time applications.
- **Offline Functionality:**
  - Apps can continue to function even without an internet connection.
  - This is beneficial for users in areas with limited connectivity.

However, on-device AI also has its limitations:

- **Limited Resources:**
  - Mobile devices have less processing power and memory than cloud servers.
  - This restricts the complexity of models that can be run on-device.
- **Model Size:**

- Large models may not fit on devices or may consume excessive resources.

Practical Implementation (TensorFlow Lite):

Kotlin

```
import android.content.res.AssetManager

import org.tensorflow.lite.Interpreter

import java.io.FileInputStream

import java.nio.ByteBuffer

import java.nio.ByteOrder

import java.nio.MappedByteBuffer

import java.nio.channels.FileChannel


class OnDeviceModel(assetManager: AssetManager) {
```

```kotlin
private var interpreter: Interpreter? = null


init {

    try {

        val model = loadModelFile(assetManager,
"your_model.tflite")

        interpreter = Interpreter(model)

    } catch (e: Exception) {

        e.printStackTrace()

    }

}


private fun loadModelFile(assetManager: AssetManager,
modelPath: String): MappedByteBuffer {

    val fileDescriptor = assetManager.openFd(modelPath)
```

```kotlin
        val inputStream =
FileInputStream(fileDescriptor.fileDescriptor)

        val fileChannel = inputStream.channel

        val startOffset = fileDescriptor.startOffset

        val declaredLength = fileDescriptor.declaredLength

        return
fileChannel.map(FileChannel.MapMode.READ_ONLY,
startOffset, declaredLength)

    }

    fun runInference(inputData: FloatArray): FloatArray? {

        interpreter?.let {

        val inputBuffer =
ByteBuffer.allocateDirect(inputData.size * 4) // Float = 4 bytes

            inputBuffer.order(ByteOrder.nativeOrder())

            inputData.forEach { inputBuffer.putFloat(it) }

            inputBuffer.rewind()
```

```
        val outputBuffer = FloatArray(10) // Example output
size

        interpreter?.run(inputBuffer, outputBuffer)

        return outputBuffer

    }

    return null

  }

}
```

Cloud-Based AI: Power from Afar

Cloud-based AI runs machine learning models on remote servers. This offers its own set of advantages:

- **Powerful Processing:**
  - Access to powerful servers allows for complex models and large datasets.
  - This is ideal for tasks that require significant computational resources.
- **Complex Models:**
  - Can handle larger, more sophisticated models.

However, cloud-based AI also has its drawbacks:

- **Privacy Concerns:**
  - Data is sent to the cloud, raising concerns about data privacy.
    -

-

- **Latency:**
  - Network latency can impact performance.
- **Connectivity Dependency:**
  - Requires a stable internet connection.

Practical Implementation (Retrofit with a Cloud API):

Kotlin

```
import retrofit2.Call

import retrofit2.Retrofit

import retrofit2.converter.gson.GsonConverterFactory

import retrofit2.http.Body

import retrofit2.http.POST
```

```kotlin
interface CloudApiService {

    @POST("predict")

    fun predict(@Body input: PredictionRequest):
Call<PredictionResponse>

}


data class PredictionRequest(val inputData: FloatArray)

data class PredictionResponse(val prediction: FloatArray)


object CloudApi {

    private const val BASE_URL = "YOUR_API_URL"


    val retrofit: CloudApiService by lazy {

        Retrofit.Builder()

            .baseUrl(BASE_URL)
```

```
.addConverterFactory(GsonConverterFactory.create())

    .build()

    .create(CloudApiService::class.java)

    }

}
```

Hybrid Approach: Best of Both Worlds

In many cases, a hybrid approach is the most effective. On-device AI can handle real-time, privacy-sensitive tasks, while cloud-based AI can handle complex, resource-intensive operations.

My Take:

I've found that the best approach often depends on the specific use case. For tasks like real-time object detection or voice commands, on-device AI is essential. For tasks like complex natural language processing or image generation, cloud-based AI may be necessary. And often, a combination of both provides the most optimal solution.

1.3 Ethical Considerations and Responsible AI

Let's talk about something that's just as important as the code we write: the ethical implications of our AI applications. We're building powerful tools, and it's our responsibility to use them wisely. Let's delve into the key ethical considerations and explore how to build responsible AI for Android.

The Power and the Responsibility

AI has the potential to transform our lives, but it also raises important ethical questions. We need to be mindful of the impact our AI apps have on users and society as a whole.

Key Ethical Considerations:

- **Bias:**
    - AI models can inherit biases from the data they're trained on.
    - This can lead to unfair or discriminatory outcomes.
    - **Example:** A facial recognition app that performs poorly on certain skin tones.
    - **My take:** Bias is like a ghost in the machine. It can be subtle, but its effects can be profound. We

need to be vigilant in identifying and mitigating bias in our models.

- **Privacy:**
  - AI apps often collect and process user data.
  - We must protect user privacy and ensure transparency.
  - **Example:** An app that collects user location data without explicit consent.
  - **My take:** Privacy is a fundamental human right. We need to respect user data and build apps that prioritize privacy.

- **Fairness:**
  - AI should be used to create fair and equitable outcomes.
  - We must avoid perpetuating existing inequalities.
  - **Example:** An AI-powered loan application that discriminates against certain demographics.
  - **My take:** Fairness is about building a level playing field. We need to ensure that our AI apps treat everyone equally.

- **Transparency:**
  - Users should understand how AI is used in their apps.

- We must be transparent about the limitations and potential biases of our models.
- **Example:** An app that uses AI to generate content should clearly disclose this to users.
- **My take:** Transparency builds trust. We need to be open and honest about how our AI apps work.

- **Accountability:**
  - Who is responsible when an AI system makes a mistake?
  - We need to establish clear lines of accountability.

Practical Steps for Responsible AI:

1. **Data Auditing:**
   - Carefully examine your training data for potential biases.
   - Use diverse and representative datasets.
   - Example: if using a dataset of images, make sure that the dataset contains a wide variety of skin tones, and ages.
2. **Model Evaluation:**

- Evaluate your models for fairness and accuracy across different demographic groups.
- Use metrics that measure fairness, such as equal opportunity and demographic parity.

3. **Privacy-Preserving Techniques:**
   - Use techniques like federated learning and differential privacy to protect user data.
   - Example: When training a model on user data, only send model updates to the cloud, not raw data.

4. **Clear Communication:**
   - Explain to users how your AI app works and how their data is used.
   - Provide clear and easy-to-understand privacy policies.

5. **Ethical Guidelines:**
   - Follow established ethical guidelines for AI development.
   - Google provides resources and best practices for responsible AI.
   - Example: Adhere to Google's AI principles.

6. **Input sanitization:**

- When dealing with user input, sanitize that input to prevent malicious code injection.
- Example: when using user provided text as a prompt for a generative ai model, ensure that the text does not contain malicious code.

7. **Regular Audits:**
   - Perform regular security audits to find and fix potential issues.
   - Stay informed of the latest security best practices.

Code Example (Privacy-Preserving Data Handling):

Kotlin

```kotlin
// Example of hashing sensitive data before sending it to a server

import java.security.MessageDigest


fun hashData(data: String): String {

    val bytes = data.toByteArray()

    val md = MessageDigest.getInstance("SHA-256")
```

```kotlin
    val digest = md.digest(bytes)

    return digest.fold("") { str, it -> str + "%02x".format(it) }

}

// Example Usage

val sensitiveData = "user_password"

val hashedData = hashData(sensitiveData)

// Send hashedData to server instead of sensitiveData
```

Key Takeaways:

- Ethical considerations are essential for building trustworthy AI apps.
- We have a responsibility to use AI for good.
- Privacy, fairness, and transparency are crucial.

Chapter 2: Setting Up Your AI Development Environment

It's time to roll up our sleeves and get our development environment ready. Building amazing AI apps starts with having the right tools and setup. This chapter will walk you through configuring Android Studio, installing the necessary SDKs, and enabling hardware acceleration. Let's make sure we're all on the same page.

2.1 Android Studio Configuration for AI

We're about to transform Android Studio into our AI-powered workshop. It's not just about writing code; it's about having the right tools and settings in place. Let's get started.

The Foundation: Latest Android Studio and SDK

The first step is ensuring we're working with the most up-to-date tools.

- **Latest Android Studio:**
    - Google constantly updates Android Studio with new features, bug fixes, and performance improvements, especially in the AI domain.

- Go to "Help" -> "Check for Updates" to ensure you're running the latest version.
- Why it matters: Newer versions often have better support for TensorFlow Lite, Gemini SDK, and other AI libraries.
- My take: Keeping Android Studio updated is like regularly servicing your car. It ensures everything runs smoothly and efficiently.

- **Target SDK:**
  - Ensure your project's target SDK is compatible with the AI libraries you plan to use.
  - Generally, targeting the latest stable SDK is recommended.
  - Why it matters: Newer SDKs often have better performance and compatibility with modern AI features.
  - My take: Targeting a modern SDK is like building on a solid foundation. It ensures your app can leverage the latest advancements.

Project Setup and Dependencies

Next, let's set up our project and add the necessary dependencies.

- **New Project or Existing:**
  - Create a new Android project or open an existing one.
  - Ensure the project is set up for Kotlin or Java, depending on your preference.
- **build.gradle (Module :app):**
  - This is where we'll add the dependencies for TensorFlow Lite, Gemini SDK, and other AI libraries.
  - Tensorflow Lite implementation.
- Gradle

```
dependencies {

    implementation 'org.tensorflow:tensorflow-lite:+'

    implementation 'org.tensorflow:tensorflow-lite-gpu:+'
//Optional for GPU support
```

```
//other dependancies
```

```
}
```

- o Gemini SDK implementation.
  - ■ At the time of writing, the Gemini SDK is under active development. Ensure to check the most up to date Google developer resources for the correct implementation.
- o MediaPipe Implementation.
  - ■ The MediaPipe implementation will vary based on your intended use case. Refer to the MediaPipe documentation for the most accurate implementation.
- **Why it matters:** Dependencies provide access to pre-built libraries and tools, saving us time and effort.
- My take: Dependencies are like building blocks. They provide the essential components we need to build our AI apps.

Hardware Acceleration: GPU and NPU

To get the best performance from our AI models, we need to leverage hardware acceleration.

- **GPU Acceleration:**
  - Modern Android devices have powerful GPUs that can significantly speed up ML inference.
  - TensorFlow Lite supports GPU acceleration through delegates.
  - Ensure the device you're testing on supports GPU delegation.
  - How to enable GPU delegation.

```
import org.tensorflow.lite.Interpreter

import org.tensorflow.lite.gpu.CompatibilityList

import org.tensorflow.lite.gpu.GpuDelegate1

    fun createInterpreter(modelFile: String, assetManager:
    android.content.res.AssetManager): Interpreter? {

        val compatList = CompatibilityList()
```

```kotlin
val options = Interpreter.Options().apply {

    if (compatList.isDelegateSupportedOnThisDevice)
    {

        // if the device has a supported GPU, add the
        GPU delegate

        val delegateOptions = GpuDelegate.Options()

this.addDelegate(GpuDelegate(delegateOptions))

    } else {

        // if the GPU is not supported, run on the CPU

        numThreads = 4

    }
```

```
    }

    try {

        val model = loadModelFile(assetManager,
modelFile)

        return Interpreter(model, options)

    } catch (e: Exception) {

        e.printStackTrace()

    }

    return null

}

```
```
```

- **NPU Acceleration:**
  - Some devices have dedicated Neural Processing Units (NPUs) optimized for AI tasks.
  - NPU support in Android is evolving. Check the device manufacturer's documentation and the latest Android developer resources.
  - TensorFlow Lite can utilize NPUs when available.
- **Emulator vs. Real Device:**
  - For optimal performance testing, use a real device with GPU or NPU support.
  - The Android emulator may not accurately reflect real-world performance.
  - Many emulators do not have proper GPU support.
- **Why it matters:** Hardware acceleration can significantly improve the speed and efficiency of our AI apps.
- My take: Hardware acceleration is like adding a turbocharger to your engine. It gives your AI apps a significant performance boost.

Key Considerations:

- Always refer to the official documentation for the latest installation instructions and best practices.

- Test your setup on multiple devices to ensure compatibility.
- Keep your development tools up to date.

2.2 Essential SDKs and Dependencies (TensorFlow Lite, Gemini SDK, etc.)

Now that our Android Studio environment is primed, let's talk about the essential SDKs and dependencies that will power our AI apps. Think of these as the building blocks that enable us to bring powerful AI capabilities to our Android creations.

TensorFlow Lite: On-Device Machine Learning Powerhouse

TensorFlow Lite is our go-to library for running machine learning models on Android devices. It's optimized for mobile and embedded systems, allowing us to build fast and efficient AI apps.

- **Why it's essential:**
  - Runs ML models directly on-device, enabling real-time inference.
  - Optimized for mobile performance, reducing latency and resource usage.

- Supports various model types, including image classification, object detection, and NLP.
- **Implementation:**
  - Add the TensorFlow Lite dependency to your build.gradle (Module :app) file:

Gradle

```
dependencies {

    implementation 'org.tensorflow:tensorflow-lite:+'

    implementation 'org.tensorflow:tensorflow-lite-gpu:+' // Optional for GPU support

    // Other dependencies...

}
```

- **My take:** TensorFlow Lite is like a finely tuned engine for on-device AI. It allows us to bring the power of machine learning to our Android apps without sacrificing performance.

Gemini SDK: Generative AI at Your Fingertips

The Gemini SDK provides access to Google's Gemini models, enabling us to integrate generative AI capabilities into our Android apps.

- **Why it's essential:**
    - Allows us to generate text, images, and other creative content.
    - Enables the development of multimodal AI applications.
    - Provides access to Google's cutting-edge generative AI models.
- **Implementation:**
    - At the time of writing, the Gemini SDK is under active development. Ensure to check the most up to date Google developer resources for the correct implementation.
    - Google will provide the latest implementation instructions and best practices.
- **My take:** The Gemini SDK is like a creative toolkit. It opens up new possibilities for building AI-powered apps that generate unique and engaging content.

MediaPipe: Real-Time Computer Vision and More

MediaPipe is a framework for building multimodal applied machine learning pipelines. It's particularly useful for computer vision tasks like pose estimation and gesture recognition.

- **Why it's essential:**
  - Provides pre-built solutions for common computer vision tasks.
  - Enables real-time processing of video and audio data.
  - Supports cross-platform development.
- **Implementation:**
  - The MediaPipe implementation will vary based on your intended use case. Refer to the MediaPipe documentation for the most accurate implementation.
  - MediaPipe has native libraries, and the implementation will depend on the features you want to use.
- **My take:** MediaPipe is like a Swiss Army knife for computer vision. It provides a wide range of tools for building sophisticated vision-based applications.

Other Essential Libraries:

- **Retrofit:** For making network requests to cloud-based AI APIs.
- **Gson:** For parsing JSON data from cloud APIs.
- **CameraX:** For handling camera access and image processing.
- **AndroidX Libraries:** For various UI and utility functions.

Key Considerations:

- Always refer to the official documentation for the latest installation instructions and best practices.
- Keep your dependencies up to date to ensure compatibility and security.
- Choose the right libraries for your specific AI tasks.

2.3 Hardware Acceleration (GPU, NPU) Setup

Hey developers! We've got our tools ready, now let's crank up the speed. Hardware acceleration is key to running our AI models efficiently on Android devices. Let's dive into setting up GPU and NPU acceleration.

The Need for Speed: Hardware Acceleration

Mobile devices have limited resources, so we need to leverage their hardware capabilities to run AI models smoothly. GPUs and NPUs are our allies in this endeavor.

- **GPU (Graphics Processing Unit):**
    - Modern Android devices have powerful GPUs that can significantly accelerate ML inference.
    - GPUs are designed for parallel processing, making them ideal for matrix operations, which are fundamental to ML.
    - TensorFlow Lite can utilize GPUs through delegates.
- **NPU (Neural Processing Unit):**
    - Some devices have dedicated NPUs optimized for AI tasks.
    - NPUs are specifically designed for neural network computations.
    - NPU support in Android is evolving, and availability varies across devices.

Setting Up GPU Acceleration with TensorFlow Lite

Let's walk through the steps to enable GPU acceleration in our TensorFlow Lite models.

1. **Add GPU Dependency:**
   - Ensure you have the GPU dependency in your build.gradle (Module :app) file:

Gradle

```
dependencies {

    implementation 'org.tensorflow:tensorflow-lite:+'

    implementation 'org.tensorflow:tensorflow-lite-gpu:+' // Enable GPU support

    // other dependencies

}
```

2. **Create Interpreter with GPU Delegate:**
   - Use the GpuDelegate to enable GPU acceleration.
   - Use the CompatibilityList to check if a GPU delegate is supported on the device.

Kotlin

```kotlin
import org.tensorflow.lite.Interpreter

import org.tensorflow.lite.gpu.CompatibilityList

import org.tensorflow.lite.gpu.GpuDelegate


fun createTfliteInterpreter(modelFile: String, assetManager:
android.content.res.AssetManager): Interpreter? {

    val compatList = CompatibilityList()

    val options = Interpreter.Options().apply {

        if (compatList.isDelegateSupportedOnThisDevice) {

            // If the device has a supported GPU, add the GPU
delegate

            val delegateOptions = GpuDelegate.Options()

            this.addDelegate(GpuDelegate(delegateOptions))

        } else {

            // If the GPU is not supported, run on the CPU
```

```
        numThreads = 4

    }

}

try {

    val model = loadModelFile(assetManager, modelFile)

    return Interpreter(model, options)

} catch (e: Exception) {

    e.printStackTrace()

}

return null

}
```

3. **Load the Model:**

   o use the helper function loadModelFile from
      previous examples to load the .tflite model.

NPU Acceleration: Device-Specific Considerations

NPU acceleration is more device-specific. Here's what you need to know:

- **Device Compatibility:**
  - NPU support varies across Android devices.
  - Check the device manufacturer's documentation for NPU compatibility.

- **TensorFlow Lite Delegates:**
  - TensorFlow Lite can utilize NPUs through delegates, but support is still evolving.
  - Refer to the TensorFlow Lite documentation for the latest NPU delegate information.

- **Manufacturer SDKs:**
  - Some device manufacturers provide their own SDKs for NPU acceleration.
  - These SDKs may offer better performance than generic NPU delegates.

Emulator vs. Real Device: Performance Matters

- **Real Device Testing:**
  - Always test your AI apps on real devices with GPU or NPU support.

- The Android emulator may not accurately reflect real-world performance.
- Many emulators do not support gpu acceleration.
- **Performance Benchmarking:**
  - Use the Tensorflow lite benchmark tool to measure the performance of your models on target hardware.

My Take:

I've found that using hardware acceleration is like unlocking a hidden potential in our Android devices. It can dramatically improve the performance of our AI apps, especially for real-time applications.

Key Considerations:

- Test your apps on a variety of devices to ensure compatibility.
- Stay up-to-date with the latest TensorFlow Lite and device manufacturer documentation.
- Prioritize real device testing for accurate performance evaluation.

Chapter 3: On-Device ML Essentials

Now that our development environment is set up, let's talk about the core techniques that make on-device ML possible. We're going to explore model optimization, latency management, and data preprocessing. These are the secret ingredients that turn bulky cloud models into sleek, efficient Android apps.

3.1 Model Optimization Techniques (Quantization, Pruning)

We've got our models, but they're often too big and slow for mobile devices. That's where model optimization comes in. Let's explore two key techniques: Quantization and Pruning.

The Need for Optimization: Mobile Constraints

Mobile devices have limited resources: processing power, memory, and battery life. We need to optimize our models to fit within these constraints.

Quantization: Reducing Precision, Reducing Size

Quantization is like compressing a high-resolution image into a smaller file. We reduce the precision of the model's weights and activations, typically from 32-bit floating-point numbers (float32) to 8-bit integers (int8).

- **How it works:**
  - Converts floating-point numbers to integers, reducing the number of bits required to store them.
  - This reduces model size and speeds up inference.
- **Benefits:**
  - Reduced model size (up to 4x reduction).
  - Faster inference speed.
  - Lower memory usage.
- **TensorFlow Lite Support:**
  - TensorFlow Lite provides various quantization techniques, including post-training quantization and quantization-aware training.
- **Post-Training Quantization Example (Kotlin):**

Kotlin

```
import org.tensorflow.lite.Interpreter
```

```
import org.tensorflow.lite.support.common.FileUtil

import org.tensorflow.lite.support.common.TensorProcessor

import
org.tensorflow.lite.support.common.ops.NormalizeOp

import org.tensorflow.lite.support.tensorbuffer.TensorBuffer

import
org.tensorflow.lite.support.quantization.schema.QuantizationP
arams

import
org.tensorflow.lite.support.quantization.QuantizationFlag



fun quantizeTfliteModel(modelFile: String, assetManager:
android.content.res.AssetManager): Interpreter? {

    try {

        val modelBuffer =
FileUtil.loadMappedFile(assetManager, modelFile)

        val options = Interpreter.Options()

        options.setQuantization(true);
```

```
        return Interpreter(modelBuffer, options)

    } catch (e: Exception) {

        e.printStackTrace()

        return null

    }

}
```

- **My take:** Quantization is like a magic trick. It dramatically reduces model size without significantly impacting accuracy.

Pruning: Trimming the Fat

Pruning is like trimming the branches of a tree to make it more compact. We remove unnecessary connections (weights) from the model.

- **How it works:**
    - Removes weights that have a value close to zero.
    - Reduces model complexity and size.
- **Benefits:**

- ○ Reduced model size.
- ○ Faster inference speed.
- ○ Lower computational requirements.
- **TensorFlow Lite Support:**
  - ○ TensorFlow Lite provides tools for pruning models during training.
- **Pruning during training (Conceptual Explanation):**
  - ○ Pruning is generally performed during the model training process, using Tensorflow Keras.
  - ○ The tensorflow model optimization toolkit contains the needed functions.
  - ○ Example: using the tfmot.sparsity.keras.prune_low_magnitude function.
- **My take:** Pruning is like a sculptor chipping away at a block of marble to reveal the essential form.

Practical Considerations:

- **Accuracy Trade-offs:**
  - ○ Optimization techniques can sometimes reduce model accuracy.

- Experiment with different techniques and parameters to find the best balance between size, speed, and accuracy.

- **Hardware Compatibility:**
  - Ensure your optimized models are compatible with the target Android devices.
  - Test your models on a variety of devices.

- **Quantization Aware Training:**
  - For best accuracy, use quantization aware training. This method trains the model with quantization in mind.

Key Takeaways:

- Quantization and pruning are essential for on-device model optimization.
- These techniques can significantly reduce model size and improve performance.
- Experiment with different optimization strategies to find the best results for your specific use case.

3.2 Efficient Model Inference and Latency Management

We've optimized our models, but now we need to ensure they run quickly and efficiently on Android devices. Let's delve into the techniques for managing inference and minimizing latency.

The Need for Speed: Real-Time Responsiveness

Users expect instant feedback, especially in real-time applications. High latency can lead to a poor user experience. We need to optimize our inference pipeline to minimize delays.

Key Techniques for Latency Management:

1. **Thread Management:**
   - **Asynchronous Inference:**
     - Run inference on a background thread to prevent blocking the main UI thread.
     - This ensures a smooth and responsive user interface.
   - **TensorFlow Lite Async API:**
     - TensorFlow Lite provides asynchronous APIs for running inference.
   - **Code Example (Kotlin):**

Kotlin

```kotlin
import kotlinx.coroutines.*

import org.tensorflow.lite.Interpreter


fun runInferenceAsync(interpreter: Interpreter,
inputData: FloatArray, outputBuffer: FloatArray,
callback: (FloatArray) -> Unit) {

    CoroutineScope(Dispatchers.IO).launch {

        val inputBuffer =
ByteBuffer.allocateDirect(inputData.size * 4) // Float =
4 bytes

        inputBuffer.order(ByteOrder.nativeOrder())

        inputData.forEach { inputBuffer.putFloat(it) }
```

```
inputBuffer.rewind()

interpreter.run(inputBuffer, outputBuffer)

withContext(Dispatchers.Main) {

  callback(outputBuffer)

}

}

}
```

2. **Hardware Acceleration (Recap):**
   - ○ **GPU and NPU Delegation:**
     - ■ Leverage GPUs and NPUs for faster inference.
     - ■ As discussed in section 2.3, use TensorFlow Lite delegates to enable hardware acceleration.
   - ○

- Benefits:
  - Significant speed improvements, especially for large models.

3. **Model Caching:**
   - **Load Once, Reuse Often:**
     - Load the model once and cache it in memory.
     - Avoid reloading the model for every inference.
   - **Benefits:**
     - Reduces initialization overhead.

4. **Input Batching:**
   - **Process Multiple Inputs Simultaneously:**
     - When possible, process multiple inputs at once to improve throughput.
     - This is useful for tasks like image processing, where you can process multiple frames in a batch.
   - **Benefits:**
     - Improved efficiency for batch processing.

5. **Data Preprocessing Optimization:**
    - **Minimize Preprocessing Overhead:**
        - Optimize data preprocessing steps to reduce latency.
        - Avoid unnecessary computations and memory allocations.
    - **Example:** If resizing images, use efficient resizing algorithms.

6. **Model Profiling:**
    - **Identify Bottlenecks:**
        - Use profiling tools to identify performance bottlenecks in your model and inference pipeline.
        - Tensorflow lite benchmark tool, and Android studio profiler are very useful.
    - **Iterative Improvement:**
        - Iteratively optimize your model and code based on profiling results.

Practical Considerations:

- **Real-Time vs. Non-Real-Time Applications:**
  - The latency requirements vary depending on the application.
  - Real-time applications (e.g., camera filters) require extremely low latency.
- **Device Variations:**
  - Performance can vary across different Android devices.
  - Test your app on a variety of devices.
- **Power Consumption:**
  - High-performance inference can consume significant power.
  - Balance performance and power consumption.

My Take:

I've found that efficient latency management is like fine-tuning an engine. It requires careful attention to detail and a deep understanding of the underlying processes. By optimizing our inference pipeline, we can create smooth and responsive AI experiences for our users.

3.3 Data Handling and Preprocessing for On-Device Models

We've got our optimized models running smoothly, but they're only as good as the data we feed them. Let's delve into the essential techniques for data handling and preprocessing on Android.

The Importance of Clean and Consistent Data

On-device models are sensitive to the quality and format of input data. Proper preprocessing ensures that our models receive consistent and relevant data, leading to better predictions.

Key Techniques for Data Handling and Preprocessing:

1. **Data Normalization:**
   - **Scaling Data to a Consistent Range:**
     - Scale input data to a consistent range, typically between 0 and 1 or -1 and 1.
     - This improves model stability and performance.

- ○ **Code Example (Kotlin):**

Kotlin

```kotlin
fun normalizeData(data: FloatArray, minValue: Float,
maxValue: Float): FloatArray {

    val range = maxValue - minValue

    return data.map { (it - minValue) / range }.toFloatArray()

}
```

2. **Image Resizing and Cropping:**
   - ○ **Matching Model Input Size:**
     - ■ Resize images to the input size expected by the model.
     - ■ Crop relevant regions of interest.
   - ○ **Code Example (Kotlin):**

Kotlin

```kotlin
import android.graphics.Bitmap

import android.graphics.Matrix
```

```kotlin
fun resizeBitmap(bitmap: Bitmap, width: Int, height: Int):
Bitmap {

    return Bitmap.createScaledBitmap(bitmap, width, height,
true)

}




fun cropBitmap(bitmap: Bitmap, x: Int, y: Int, width: Int,
height: Int): Bitmap {

    return Bitmap.createBitmap(bitmap, x, y, width, height)

}
```

3. **Text Tokenization:**
   - **Converting Text to Numerical Tokens:**
     - Convert text into numerical tokens that the model can understand.
     - TensorFlow Lite supports various tokenization techniques.
   - **TensorFlow Lite Support:**

- Tensorflow lite has support libraries for text processing, including tokenization.
  - **Code Concept (Conceptual):**
    - Use Tensorflow lite support libraries to tokenize input text.

4. **Data Augmentation (During Training):**
   - **Increasing Data Variety:**
     - Apply random transformations to the training data to increase its variety.
     - This improves model generalization.
   - **Conceptual Explanation:**
     - Data augmentation is generally applied during model training, using Tensorflow Keras.
     - Example transformations: random rotations, flips, and zooms.

5. **Efficient Data Loading:**
   - **Minimize I/O Overhead:**
     - Load data efficiently to reduce I/O overhead.
     - Use asynchronous data loading when possible.

- Example: Use BitmapFactory.Options to load images efficiently.

6. **Data Caching:**
   - **Store Preprocessed Data:**
     - Cache preprocessed data to avoid redundant computations.
     - Use in-memory caches or disk caches.

Practical Considerations:

- **Model Input Requirements:**
  - Always check the model's input requirements to ensure you're providing data in the correct format.
- **Performance Trade-offs:**
  - Preprocessing can add overhead, so optimize for speed.
- **Data Consistency:**
  - Ensure that preprocessing is consistent across training and inference.

My Take:

I've found that data preprocessing is like preparing ingredients for a recipe. The better you prepare them, the better the final dish will taste. By carefully preprocessing our data, we can significantly improve the performance and accuracy of our on-device models.

Chapter 4: Computer Vision with On-Device Models

Get ready to open your eyes to the world of computer vision. We're going to explore how to make our Android apps "see" and understand images and videos, all while keeping things running smoothly on-device. Let's get started!

4.1 Image Classification and Object Detection (TensorFlow Lite)

We're about to make our Android apps visually intelligent. Image classification and object detection are fundamental computer vision tasks, and TensorFlow Lite makes them accessible on mobile devices. Let's get started.

Image Classification: What's in the Image?

Image classification involves identifying the main object or scene in an image.

- **How it works:**
  - A pre-trained model analyzes the image and assigns it to a category.

- TensorFlow Lite allows us to run these models on Android.
- **Practical Implementation (Kotlin):**

Kotlin

```kotlin
import android.content.res.AssetManager

import android.graphics.Bitmap

import android.graphics.BitmapFactory

import org.tensorflow.lite.Interpreter

import org.tensorflow.lite.support.common.FileUtil

import org.tensorflow.lite.support.common.TensorProcessor
```

```kotlin
import
org.tensorflow.lite.support.common.ops.Normaliz
eOp


import
org.tensorflow.lite.support.image.TensorImage




class ImageClassifier(assetManager:
AssetManager, modelFile: String, private val
imageSize: Int) {




    private var interpreter: Interpreter? = null
```

```kotlin
init {

    try {

        val model =
        FileUtil.loadMappedFile(assetManager,
        modelFile)

        interpreter = Interpreter(model)

    } catch (e: Exception) {

        e.printStackTrace()

    }

}
```

```kotlin
fun classifyImage(bitmap: Bitmap):
FloatArray? {


    interpreter?.let {


        val tensorImage =
TensorImage.fromBitmap(resizeBitmap(bitmap,
imageSize, imageSize))


        val imageProcessor =
TensorProcessor.Builder().add(NormalizeOp(0f,
255f)).build()


        val processedImage =
imageProcessor.process(tensorImage)
```

```kotlin
        val outputBuffer = FloatArray(1001) //
Adjust based on your model's output


        interpreter?.run(processedImage.buffer,
outputBuffer)


        return outputBuffer


    }


        return null


    }




    private fun resizeBitmap(bitmap: Bitmap,
width: Int, height: Int): Bitmap {
```

```
        return Bitmap.createScaledBitmap(bitmap,
width, height, true)



    }



  }




  // Example Usage:



  // val classifier = ImageClassifier(assets,
"mobilenet_v1_1.0_224.tflite", 224)



  // val bitmap =
BitmapFactory.decodeResource(resources,
R.drawable.my_image)
```

```
// val results = classifier.classifyImage(bitmap)
```

- **Key Points:**
  - imageSize must match your model's input size.
  - The outputBuffer size depends on the number of classes your model predicts.
  - Normalize the input image to the model's expected range.

Object Detection: Where Are the Objects?

Object detection goes beyond classification, locating objects within an image using bounding boxes.

- **How it works:**
  - The model outputs bounding box coordinates and class labels.
  - TensorFlow Lite supports models like SSD MobileNet for object detection.
- **Practical Implementation (Kotlin - Conceptual):**

Kotlin

```
// Conceptual Example (Object Detection):


// The outputs of an object detection model are
more complex.


// They typically include bounding boxes, class
labels, and confidence scores.


// Example of how to process the output of a
detection model.


// The actual code will vary greatly based on
the model.




// Example of the type of outputs a detection
model will return.
```

```
// Float array that contains bounding box
coordinates, class labels, and confidence scores.


fun processDetectionOutput(outputBuffer:
FloatArray) {


    // Parse the outputBuffer to extract bounding
boxes, class labels, and confidence scores.


    // Draw the bounding boxes on the image.


}


// Example Usage.


// val detector = ObjectDetector(assets,
"ssd_mobilenet_v1_1_metadata_1.tflite", 300);
```

```
// val results = detector.detectObjects(bitmap);
```

```
// processDetectionOutput(results);
```

- **Key Points:**
  - ○ Object detection models have more complex outputs than classification models.
  - ○ You'll need to parse the output buffer to extract the relevant information.
  - ○ Use drawing functions to display the bounding boxes on the image.

Practical Considerations:

- **Model Selection:**
  - ○ Choose models that are optimized for mobile devices.
  - ○ MobileNet and EfficientNet are popular choices for image classification.
  - ○ SSD MobileNet is a common choice for object detection.
  - ○

- **Performance Optimization:**
    - Use hardware acceleration (GPU, NPU) for faster inference.
    - Quantize your models to reduce size and improve performance.
- **Real-Time Processing:**
    - For real-time applications, optimize your code to minimize latency.
    - Use asynchronous inference and efficient data preprocessing.

My Take:

I've found that image classification and object detection can add a whole new dimension to Android apps. They allow us to build apps that can understand and interact with the visual world around us. By using Tensorflow lite, we can bring these capabilities to our users, while respecting their privacy.

4.2 Pose Estimation and Gesture Recognition (MediaPipe)

We're about to make our Android apps more interactive by enabling them to understand human poses and gestures. MediaPipe is a powerful tool for these tasks, and let's see how we can leverage it.

Pose Estimation: Understanding Human Movement

Pose estimation involves identifying key points on the human body, such as joints and limbs.

- **How it works:**
  - MediaPipe provides pre-trained models that can detect these key points from images or video streams.
  - This allows us to track human movement in real-time.
- **Practical Implementation (Kotlin - Conceptual):**

Kotlin

```
// Conceptual Example (Pose Estimation):

// MediaPipe requires native libraries.
```

// The implementation will vary based on the specific pose estimation model used.

// Example of how to initialize MediaPipe and process frames.


```kotlin
import com.google.mediapipe.formats.proto.landmark.NormalizedLandmarkListProto.NormalizedLandmarkList

import com.google.mediapipe.components.FrameProcessor

import com.google.mediapipe.framework.AndroidAssetUtil

import com.google.mediapipe.framework.PacketGetter

import com.google.mediapipe.glutil.EglManager


class PoseEstimator(context: android.content.Context,
private val listener: (NormalizedLandmarkList) -> Unit) {
```

```kotlin
private val eglManager = EglManager(null)

private val processor = FrameProcessor(

    context,

    eglManager.nativeContext,

    "pose_landmark_gpu.binarypb", // Example graph

    "input_video",

    "output_landmarks"

)


init {


AndroidAssetUtil.initializeNativeAssetManager(context)

    processor.videoInputStream.setListener { packet ->

    val landmarks = PacketGetter.getProto(packet,
NormalizedLandmarkList.getDefaultInstance())

        listener(landmarks)
```

```kotlin
        }

    }


    fun processFrame(bitmap: android.graphics.Bitmap,
timestamp: Long) {


processor.send(com.google.mediapipe.formats.proto.image.Im
ageProtoUtil.createProto(bitmap), timestamp)

    }


    fun close() {

        processor.close()

        eglManager.release()

    }

}


// Example Usage:
```

```
// val poseEstimator = PoseEstimator(this) { landmarks ->

//     // Process the landmarks here.

//     // Draw the landmarks on the screen.

// }

// poseEstimator.processFrame(bitmap, System.nanoTime() /
1000);
```

- **Key Points:**
  - MediaPipe requires native libraries, so integration can be complex.
  - The FrameProcessor handles the processing of video frames.
  - The NormalizedLandmarkList contains the detected key points.

Gesture Recognition: Interpreting Human Actions

Gesture recognition builds on pose estimation, allowing us to interpret human actions.

- **How it works:**
  - We analyze the detected key points to recognize specific gestures, such as waving or clapping.

○ MediaPipe provides tools for building custom gesture recognition systems.

- **Practical Implementation (Kotlin - Conceptual):**

Kotlin

```
// Conceptual Example (Gesture Recognition):

// Gesture recognition involves analyzing the landmarks to detect specific patterns.


fun recognizeGesture(landmarks: NormalizedLandmarkList): String {

    // Analyze the landmarks to identify a gesture.

    // Example: check the position of the hands to detect a wave.

    if (landmarks.landmarkCount > 0) {

        // Logic to calculate distances and positions of landmarks to determine a gesture.

        // Return a string that describes the gesture.
```

```
    }

    return "Unknown Gesture"

}


// Example Usage:

// val gesture = recognizeGesture(landmarks);
```

- **Key Points:**
    - Gesture recognition requires custom logic to analyze the landmarks.
    - You can use distances and angles between key points to identify gestures.
    - MediaPipe's solutions provide examples on how to build gesture recognizers.

Practical Considerations:

- **Performance:**
    - MediaPipe can be resource-intensive, so optimize your code for real-time performance.
    - Use hardware acceleration (GPU) when possible.
    -

- **Accuracy:**
  - Gesture recognition accuracy depends on the quality of the pose estimation and the complexity of the gestures.
  - Test your app in various lighting conditions and with different users.
- **Complexity:**
  - MediaPipe can be complex to set up, and integrate, properly read the mediapipe documentation.

My Take:

I've found that pose estimation and gesture recognition can make Android apps feel more natural and intuitive. They allow users to interact with their devices in a more human-like way.

4.3 Real-Time Vision Applications Development

We've explored image classification, object detection, pose estimation, and gesture recognition. Now, let's combine these techniques to build dynamic, real-time vision applications.

The Power of Real-Time Vision

Real-time vision allows our apps to react to the visual world as it happens, opening up possibilities for interactive and immersive experiences.

Key Techniques for Real-Time Vision:

1. **Camera Integration with CameraX:**
    - **Capturing Video Frames:**
        - Use CameraX to capture video frames from the device's camera.
        - CameraX simplifies camera access and provides a consistent API.
    - **Code Example (Kotlin):**

Kotlin

```kotlin
import androidx.camera.core.*

import androidx.camera.lifecycle.ProcessCameraProvider

import androidx.camera.view.PreviewView
```

```kotlin
import androidx.core.content.ContextCompat

import java.util.concurrent.Executors


fun setupCamera(context: android.content.Context,
previewView: PreviewView, imageAnalysis: ImageAnalysis) {

    val cameraProviderFuture =
ProcessCameraProvider.getInstance(context)

    cameraProviderFuture.addListener({

        val cameraProvider = cameraProviderFuture.get()

        val preview = Preview.Builder().build().also {

            it.setSurfaceProvider(previewView.surfaceProvider)

        }

        val cameraSelector =
CameraSelector.DEFAULT_BACK_CAMERA

        try {

            cameraProvider.unbindAll()

            cameraProvider.bindToLifecycle(
```

```kotlin
                context as androidx.lifecycle.LifecycleOwner,

                cameraSelector,

                preview,

                imageAnalysis

            )

        } catch (exc: Exception) {

            // Handle exceptions

        }

    }, ContextCompat.getMainExecutor(context))

}


fun createImageAnalysis(): ImageAnalysis {

    return ImageAnalysis.Builder()

.setBackpressureStrategy(ImageAnalysis.STRATEGY_KEEP_
ONLY_LATEST)
```

```kotlin
        .build()

        .also {


it.setAnalyzer(Executors.newSingleThreadExecutor()) {
imageProxy ->

            // Process the imageProxy here.

            imageProxy.close()

        }

    }

}


    // Example Usage:

    // val previewView =
findViewById<PreviewView>(R.id.previewView)

    // val imageAnalysis = createImageAnalysis()

    // setupCamera(this, previewView, imageAnalysis)
```

2. **Real-Time Inference:**

- Processing Frames Efficiently:
    - Run your AI models on each frame from the camera stream.
    - Optimize your code for speed to minimize latency.
- Asynchronous Processing:
    - Use asynchronous operations to avoid blocking the UI thread.

3. **Overlaying Results:**
    - **Visual Feedback:**
        - Draw bounding boxes, key points, or other visual cues on top of the camera preview.
        - This provides real-time feedback to the user.
    - **Custom Views or SurfaceView:**
        - Use custom views or SurfaceView to draw overlays.

4. **Performance Optimization:**
    - **Hardware Acceleration:**
        - Leverage GPUs and NPUs for faster inference.

- As discussed in section 2.3, use TensorFlow Lite delegates for hardware acceleration.
  - **Model Optimization:**
    - Use quantized and pruned models for smaller size and faster inference.
    - As discussed in section 3.1, use model optimization.

Practical Considerations:

- **Latency:**
  - Latency is critical for real-time applications.
  - Optimize your code and models to minimize delays.
- **Frame Rate:**
  - Maintain a smooth frame rate for a good user experience.
  - Balance performance and image quality.
- **Power Consumption:**
  - Real-time vision processing can consume significant power.
  - Optimize your code to conserve battery life.

- **Device Variations:**
  - Performance can vary across different Android devices.
  - Test your app on a variety of devices.

Example Applications:

- **Real-time object detection:**
  - Detect objects in the camera stream and display bounding boxes.
- **AR applications:**
  - Overlay virtual objects or information onto the real world.
- **Gesture-controlled interfaces:**
  - Control your app with hand gestures.
- **Real-time image filters:**
  - Apply artistic filters to the camera stream.

My Take:

I've found that real-time vision applications can be incredibly engaging and transformative. They allow us to interact with the world in new and exciting ways. By mastering these techniques, we can build truly innovative Android experiences.

Chapter 5: Natural Language Processing (NLP) on Android

We've explored how to make our Android apps "see" in the last chapter. Now, let's teach them to "understand" and "speak." NLP is a powerful tool for building intelligent and interactive apps that can process and generate human language. Let's get started.

5.1 Text Classification and Sentiment Analysis

We're about to make our Android apps linguistically intelligent. Text classification and sentiment analysis are fundamental NLP tasks, and with TensorFlow Lite, we can bring these capabilities to mobile devices. Let's get started.

Text Classification: Categorizing Text

Text classification involves assigning text to predefined categories or labels.

- **How it works:**

- A pre-trained model analyzes the text and assigns it to a category.
- TensorFlow Lite can run these models on Android.

- **Practical Implementation (Kotlin - Conceptual):**

Kotlin

```kotlin
// Conceptual Example (Text Classification):


// Tensorflow lite has support libraries for text processing.


// This example shows the general concept.


import org.tensorflow.lite.Interpreter


import
org.tensorflow.lite.support.common.FileUtil
```

```kotlin
import
org.tensorflow.lite.support.tensorbuffer.TensorBuf
fer


import
org.tensorflow.lite.support.text.TensorText


import java.nio.ByteBuffer




class TextClassifier(assetManager:
android.content.res.AssetManager, modelFile:
String) {


    private var interpreter: Interpreter? = null
```

```kotlin
init {

    try {

        val model =
FileUtil.loadMappedFile(assetManager,
modelFile)

            interpreter = Interpreter(model)

    } catch (e: Exception) {

        e.printStackTrace()

    }
```

```kotlin
    }



    fun classifyText(text: String): FloatArray? {


        interpreter?.let {


            val tensorText =
TensorText.create(listOf(text))



            val inputBuffer = tensorText.getBuffer()



            val outputBuffer =
TensorBuffer.createFixedSize(intArrayOf(1, 10),
```

```
org.tensorflow.lite.DataType.FLOAT32) // Adjust
based on your model's output


        interpreter?.run(inputBuffer,
outputBuffer.buffer)


        return outputBuffer.floatArray


    }


    return null


  }


}
```

```
// Example Usage:

// val classifier = TextClassifier(assets,
"text_classification.tflite")

// val results = classifier.classifyText("This is a
great product!")

// processClassificationResults(results) //
Custom function to handle output
```

- **Key Points:**
  - The model's input is text, which needs to be preprocessed (tokenized).
  - The outputBuffer size depends on the number of categories your model predicts.
  - Use Tensorflow lite text support libraries for tokenization.

Sentiment Analysis: Understanding Emotions

Sentiment analysis involves determining the emotional tone of text, such as positive, negative, or neutral.

- **How it works:**
    - A pre-trained model analyzes the text and assigns it a sentiment score or label.
    - TensorFlow Lite can run these models on Android.[7]
- **Practical Implementation (Kotlin - Conceptual):**

Kotlin

```
// Conceptual Example (Sentiment Analysis):



// Very similar to text classification, but the outputs represent sentiment.
```

```kotlin
class SentimentAnalyzer(assetManager:
android.content.res.AssetManager, modelFile:
String) {



    private var interpreter: Interpreter? = null



    // ... (Initialization similar to TextClassifier)



    fun analyzeSentiment(text: String):
FloatArray? {


        interpreter?.let {
```

```kotlin
// Preprocess the text and run inference.

// ... (Similar to classifyText)

val outputBuffer =
TensorBuffer.createFixedSize(intArrayOf(1, 3),
org.tensorflow.lite.DataType.FLOAT32) //
Example: positive, negative, neutral

interpreter?.run(inputBuffer,
outputBuffer.buffer)

return outputBuffer.floatArray

}

return null
```

```
        }



    }



    // Example Usage:



    // val analyzer = SentimentAnalyzer(assets,
"sentiment_analysis.tflite")



    // val sentiment =
analyzer.analyzeSentiment("I'm so happy!")



    // processSentimentResults(sentiment) //
Custom function to handle output
```

- **Key Points:**
  - The model's output represents the sentiment score or probability of each sentiment.
  - You'll need to interpret the output to determine the overall sentiment.

Practical Considerations:

- **Model Selection:**
  - Choose models that are optimized for mobile devices.
  - Consider the size and accuracy of the models.
- **Text Preprocessing:**
  - Text preprocessing is crucial for NLP tasks.
  - Tokenization, stemming, and lemmatization are common techniques.
  - Tensorflow lite support libraries are availible for text preprocessing.
- **Real-Time Processing:**
  - For real-time applications, optimize your code to minimize latency.
  - Use asynchronous inference and efficient data preprocessing.

My Take:

I've found that text classification and sentiment analysis can add a layer of intelligence to Android apps. They allow us to understand user input and provide personalized experiences. By using Tensorflow lite, we can bring these capabilities to our users, while respecting their privacy.

5.2 On-Device Language Models and Text Generation

We're about to explore the frontier of on-device language models, a challenging but incredibly rewarding area of Android development. Let's see how we can bring the power of text generation directly to our users' devices.

The Challenge and the Potential

On-device language models are challenging because they are typically large and computationally intensive. However, they offer significant benefits:

- **Privacy:** Data stays on the device.
- **Offline Functionality:** Works without an internet connection.
- **Real-Time Response:** Instant text generation.

Key Concepts and Considerations:

1. **Model Size and Optimization:**
   - **Quantization and Pruning:**
     - These techniques are essential for reducing the size of language models.
     - Quantization reduces precision, and pruning removes unnecessary connections.
     - As covered in chapter 3.1.
   - **Model Architectures:**
     - Use optimized architectures like MobileBERT or DistilBERT.
     - These models are designed for mobile devices.

2. **Inference Efficiency:**
   - **Asynchronous Inference:**
     - Run inference on a background thread to avoid blocking the UI.
     - As covered in chapter 3.2.
   - **Hardware Acceleration:**
     - Leverage GPUs and NPUs for faster inference.
     - As covered in chapter 2.3.

3. **Text Preprocessing:**

- ○ **Tokenization:**
  - ■ Convert text into numerical tokens that the model can understand.
  - ■ Tensorflow lite support libraries are availible for this.
- ○ **Vocabulary Handling:**
  - ■ Manage the model's vocabulary efficiently.
  - ■ Consider using subword tokenization to reduce vocabulary size.

4. **Text Generation Techniques:**
   - ○ **Autoregressive Models:**
     - ■ Generate text one token at a time, based on the previous tokens.
     - ■ This is a common approach for language models.
   - ○ **Sampling Strategies:**
     - ■ Use sampling strategies like top-k or top-p to control the diversity of the generated text.

5. **TensorFlow Lite Support:**
   - ○ **TensorFlow Lite Text:**
     - ■ TensorFlow Lite has support libraries for text processing.

- These libraries provide tools for tokenization and other text-related tasks.
- **Custom Operations:**
  - You may need to define custom operations for certain language model architectures.

Practical Implementation (Kotlin - Conceptual):

```kotlin
Kotlin

// Conceptual Example (On-Device Text
Generation):


// This example shows the general concept.


// The actual implementation will vary greatly
based on the model.
```

```kotlin
import org.tensorflow.lite.Interpreter

import
org.tensorflow.lite.support.common.FileUtil

import
org.tensorflow.lite.support.tensorbuffer.TensorBuffer

import
org.tensorflow.lite.support.text.TensorText

import java.nio.ByteBuffer

class TextGenerator(assetManager:
android.content.res.AssetManager, modelFile:
String) {
```

```kotlin
private var interpreter: Interpreter? = null

init {

    try {

        val model =
FileUtil.loadMappedFile(assetManager,
modelFile)

        interpreter = Interpreter(model)

    } catch (e: Exception) {

        e.printStackTrace()

    }
```

```kotlin
    }


    fun generateText(inputText: String,
maxOutputLength: Int): String? {


        interpreter?.let {


            // Tokenize the input text.


            val tensorText =
TensorText.create(listOf(inputText))


            val inputBuffer = tensorText.getBuffer()


            var generatedText = inputText
```

```kotlin
for (i in 0 until maxOutputLength) {

    // Run inference to generate the next token.

    val outputBuffer =
TensorBuffer.createFixedSize(intArrayOf(1, 1),
org.tensorflow.lite.DataType.INT32) // Example
output

        interpreter?.run(inputBuffer,
outputBuffer.buffer)

    // Decode the generated token.

    val nextToken =
outputBuffer.intArray[0]
```

```
        // Append the token to the generated
text.

        generatedText +=
decodeToken(nextToken);

        // Update the input buffer with the
generated token.

        // This is for autoregressive models.

        // ...

    }

    return generatedText;

}
```

```
        return null;



    }



    fun decodeToken(tokenId: Int): String{



        //Lookup token in vocabulary, and return
the string.



        return " "; //place holder.



    }



}



// Example Usage:
```

```
// val generator = TextGenerator(assets,
"text_generation.tflite")


// val generatedText =
generator.generateText("Once upon a time", 50)


// displayGeneratedText(generatedText) //
Custom function to display text
```

Practical Considerations:

- **Model Selection:**
  - Choose models that are optimized for on-device inference.
  - Consider the trade-offs between model size, accuracy, and latency.
- **Memory Management:**
  - Language models can consume significant memory.[11]
  - Use efficient data structures and memory management techniques.
- **User Experience:**

- Design user interfaces that provide a smooth and responsive text generation experience.
- Consider using streaming output to display generated text as it's produced.

My Take:

I've found that on-device language models are a fascinating area of research and development. They have the potential to revolutionize how we interact with our devices, enabling personalized and context-aware experiences. By mastering these techniques, we can build truly innovative Android applications.

5.3 Speech Recognition and Text-to-Speech Integration

We're about to give our Android apps the gift of hearing and speech. Speech recognition and TTS are powerful tools for building accessible and interactive applications. Let's get started.

Speech Recognition: Turning Voice into Text

Speech recognition allows our apps to convert spoken language into text.

- **How it works:**
  - Android provides built-in APIs for speech recognition.
  - These APIs use device capabilities and cloud-based services to transcribe speech.
- **Practical Implementation (Kotlin):**

```kotlin
Kotlin

import android.content.Intent

import android.speech.RecognizerIntent

import androidx.activity.result.contract.ActivityResultContracts

import androidx.appcompat.app.AppCompatActivity

import android.os.Bundle

import android.widget.Button

import android.widget.TextView
```

```kotlin
class SpeechRecognitionActivity : AppCompatActivity() {


    private lateinit var speechButton: Button

    private lateinit var resultTextView: TextView


    private val speechActivityResult =
registerForActivityResult(ActivityResultContracts.StartActivit
yForResult()) { result ->

        if (result.resultCode == RESULT_OK) {

            val data: Intent? = result.data

            val results: ArrayList<String>? =
data?.getStringArrayListExtra(RecognizerIntent.EXTRA_RES
ULTS)

            if (!results.isNullOrEmpty()) {

                resultTextView.text = results[0]

            }
```

```kotlin
        }

    }



    override fun onCreate(savedInstanceState: Bundle?) {

        super.onCreate(savedInstanceState)

        setContentView(R.layout.activity_speech_recognition)


        speechButton = findViewById(R.id.speechButton)

        resultTextView = findViewById(R.id.resultTextView)


        speechButton.setOnClickListener {

            startSpeechRecognition()

        }

    }


    private fun startSpeechRecognition() {
```

```kotlin
val intent =
Intent(RecognizerIntent.ACTION_RECOGNIZE_SPEECH).apply {

putExtra(RecognizerIntent.EXTRA_LANGUAGE_MODEL,
RecognizerIntent.LANGUAGE_MODEL_FREE_FORM)

        putExtra(RecognizerIntent.EXTRA_PROMPT,
"Speak now")

    }

    speechActivityResult.launch(intent)

  }

}
```

- **Key Points:**
  - RecognizerIntent is used to start the speech recognition activity.
  - EXTRA_LANGUAGE_MODEL and EXTRA_PROMPT are used to configure the recognition.
  - The results are returned as an ArrayList<String>.

Text-to-Speech (TTS): Turning Text into Voice

TTS allows our apps to convert text into spoken language.

- **How it works:**
    - Android provides built-in APIs for TTS.
    - These APIs use device capabilities to synthesize speech.
- **Practical Implementation (Kotlin):**

```kotlin
Kotlin

import android.speech.tts.TextToSpeech

import android.os.Bundle

import android.widget.Button

import android.widget.EditText

import androidx.appcompat.app.AppCompatActivity

import java.util.Locale


class TextToSpeechActivity : AppCompatActivity(),
TextToSpeech.OnInitListener {
```

```kotlin
private lateinit var tts: TextToSpeech

private lateinit var speakButton: Button

private lateinit var textEditText: EditText


override fun onCreate(savedInstanceState: Bundle?) {

    super.onCreate(savedInstanceState)

    setContentView(R.layout.activity_text_to_speech)


    speakButton = findViewById(R.id.speakButton)

    textEditText = findViewById(R.id.textEditText)


    tts = TextToSpeech(this, this)


    speakButton.setOnClickListener {

        val text = textEditText.text.toString()
```

```kotlin
        if (text.isNotEmpty()) {

            tts.speak(text, TextToSpeech.QUEUE_FLUSH,
null, "")

        }

    }

}


    override fun onInit(status: Int) {

        if (status == TextToSpeech.SUCCESS) {

            val result = tts.setLanguage(Locale.getDefault())

            if (result ==
TextToSpeech.LANG_MISSING_DATA || result ==
TextToSpeech.LANG_NOT_SUPPORTED) {

                // Handle language not supported

            }

        } else {

            // Handle TTS initialization failure
```

```kotlin
        }

    }



    override fun onDestroy() {

        if (::tts.isInitialized) {

            tts.stop()

            tts.shutdown()

        }

        super.onDestroy()

    }

}
```

- **Key Points:**
    - TextToSpeech is used to synthesize speech.
    - onInit() is called when the TTS engine is initialized.
    - tts.speak() is used to speak the provided text.
    - Locale is used to select the correct language.

Practical Considerations:

- **Permissions:**
  - Speech recognition requires the RECORD_AUDIO permission.
- **Language Support:**
  - Ensure that the desired languages are supported by the speech recognition and TTS engines.
- **User Experience:**
  - Provide clear feedback to the user during speech recognition and TTS.
  - Consider using visual cues to indicate that the app is listening or speaking.
- **Error Handling:**
  - Handle errors gracefully, such as network errors or unsupported languages.

My Take:

I've found that speech integration can significantly enhance the accessibility and usability of Android apps. It allows users to interact with their devices in a more natural and intuitive way. By mastering these techniques, we can build truly inclusive and engaging applications.

Chapter 6: Generative AI with the Gemini API

Welcome to the exciting realm of generative AI. We're about to dive into the Gemini API, a powerful tool that allows us to generate text, images, and more. This chapter will guide you through the basics and show you how to start building creative applications.

6.1 Introduction to Gemini Models and API

We're about to embark on a journey into the realm of Google's Gemini models. These are multimodal models designed to understand and generate content across various modalities, including text, images, and more. Let's dive in.

Gemini: A Multimodal Marvel

Gemini models represent a significant advancement in AI, offering capabilities that go beyond traditional language models.

- **Multimodal Understanding:**
  - Gemini can process and understand information from multiple sources, such as text, images, and code.
  - This allows for richer and more nuanced interactions.
- **Advanced Reasoning:**
  - Gemini is designed to perform complex reasoning tasks, enabling it to answer questions, generate creative content, and solve problems.
- **Versatile Applications:**
  - Gemini can be used for a wide range of applications, including:
    - Content creation
    - Image understanding
    - Code generation
    - And much more.

The Gemini API: Accessing the Power

The Gemini API provides developers with access to Gemini models, allowing them to integrate these capabilities into their applications.

- **API Structure:**
  - The API is designed to be flexible and easy to use.
  - It supports various input and output formats, reflecting Gemini's multimodal nature.
- **Authentication:**
  - Access to the Gemini API requires authentication.
  - Google Cloud Platform (GCP) credentials are used to authorize requests.
- **Usage Considerations:**
  - As the Gemini API is under active development, always refer to the most up to date google developer documentation for the most accurate information.

Practical Considerations (Conceptual):

- **API Integration:**
  - Integrating the Gemini API into your Android app involves making HTTP requests to the API endpoints.
  - Libraries like Retrofit can simplify this process.
- **Data Handling:**

- You'll need to handle various data formats, including text, images, and JSON.
- Gson, or other json parsing libraries will be very useful.

- **Error Handling:**
  - Implement robust error handling to manage API errors and network issues.

- **Latency:**
  - Network latency will be a factor when using the cloud based API. Optimize your code to handle potential delays.

Conceptual Code Example (Kotlin with Retrofit):

Kotlin

```
//Conceptual example. Gemini api implementation
will change.


import retrofit2.Call


import retrofit2.Retrofit
```

```kotlin
import retrofit2.converter.gson.GsonConverterFactory

import retrofit2.http.Body

import retrofit2.http.Headers

import retrofit2.http.POST

interface GeminiApiService {

    @Headers("Content-Type: application/json")

    @POST("generateContent")

    fun generateContent(@Body request:
GeminiRequest): Call<GeminiResponse>

}
```

```kotlin
data class GeminiRequest(val contents:
List<Content>)

data class Content(val parts: List<Part>)

data class Part(val text: String)

data class GeminiResponse(val candidates:
List<Candidate>)

data class Candidate(val content: Content)

object GeminiApi {

    private const val BASE_URL =
"YOUR_GEMINI_API_URL" //Replace with the
Correct Gemini API URL.

    val retrofit: GeminiApiService by lazy {

        Retrofit.Builder()
```

```
        .baseUrl(BASE_URL)


.addConverterFactory(GsonConverterFactory.create())


        .build()


        .create(GeminiApiService::class.java)


    }


    }



    //Example Usage.

    //val request =
GeminiRequest(listOf(Content(listOf(Part("Write a
poem")))))
```

```kotlin
//val call =
GeminiApi.retrofit.generateContent(request)

//call.enqueue(object :
retrofit2.Callback<GeminiResponse> {

//    override fun onResponse(call:
Call<GeminiResponse>, response:
retrofit2.Response<GeminiResponse>) {

//        //Handle response.

//    }

//    override fun onFailure(call:
Call<GeminiResponse>, t: Throwable) {

//        //Handle Failure.

//    }
```

//})

My Take:

I'm incredibly excited about the potential of Gemini models.
Their multimodal capabilities open up new avenues for
building intelligent and engaging Android applications. By
leveraging the Gemini API, we can bring these advanced AI
features to our users.

Key Considerations:

- Always refer to the official Gemini API documentation
  for the latest information and best practices.
- Pay close attention to API usage limits and pricing.
- Handle user data responsibly, and respect user privacy.

6.2 Text and Image Generation with Gemini

We're about to delve into the creative potential of Gemini
models, specifically their ability to generate text and images.
This opens up a world of possibilities for building engaging
and dynamic Android apps.

Gemini's Multimodal Generation Power

Gemini's multimodal nature allows it to generate content that seamlessly blends text and images.

- **Text Generation:**
    - Gemini can generate various forms of text, including poems, stories, code, and more.
    - It can adapt its style and tone based on the input prompt.
- **Image Generation:**
    - Gemini can generate images from text descriptions or combine text and image inputs to create new visual content.
    - This is a powerful tool for visual storytelling and content creation.
- **Combined Generation:**
    - Gemini is able to generate responses that contain both text and images, based on a combination of text and image inputs.

Practical Considerations (Conceptual):

1. **Prompt Engineering:**
   - The quality of the generated content depends heavily on the input prompt.
   - Craft clear and specific prompts to guide Gemini's generation process.

2. **Data Handling:**
   - You'll need to handle image data in various formats, such as bitmaps or encoded strings.
   - Libraries like Glide or Picasso can help with image loading and display.

3. **API Requests:**
   - Making requests to the Gemini API involves sending structured data that includes text and/or image inputs.
   - The API response will contain the generated text and/or images.

4. **Error Handling:**
   - Implement robust error handling to manage API errors, image processing errors, and other potential issues.

5. **Latency and Performance:**
   - Image generation can be computationally intensive and may introduce latency.
   - Optimize your code to handle potential delays and provide a smooth user experience.

6. **Content Filtering:**
   - Implement content filtering to ensure that the generated content is safe and appropriate.
   - The gemini API will likely have built in safety features, ensure you implement any safety recommendations from Google.

Conceptual Code Example (Kotlin with Retrofit - Combined Text and Image Generation):

Kotlin

```
//Conceptual Example. Gemini API implementation
will change.

import retrofit2.Call

import retrofit2.Retrofit
```

```
import retrofit2.converter.gson.GsonConverterFactory

import retrofit2.http.Body

import retrofit2.http.Headers

import retrofit2.http.POST

import android.graphics.Bitmap

import java.io.ByteArrayOutputStream

import android.util.Base64

interface GeminiApiService {

    @Headers("Content-Type: application/json")

    @POST("generateContent")
```

```kotlin
    fun generateContent(@Body request:
GeminiRequest): Call<GeminiResponse>


    }


    data class GeminiRequest(val contents:
List<Content>)


    data class Content(val parts: List<Part>)


    data class Part(val text: String?, val inlineData:
InlineData?)


    data class InlineData(val mimeType: String, val data:
String)


    data class GeminiResponse(val candidates:
List<Candidate>)


    data class Candidate(val content: Content)
```

```kotlin
object GeminiApi {

    private const val BASE_URL =
"YOUR_GEMINI_API_URL" //Replace with the
Correct Gemini API URL.

    val retrofit: GeminiApiService by lazy {

        Retrofit.Builder()

            .baseUrl(BASE_URL)


.addConverterFactory(GsonConverterFactory.create())

            .build()

            .create(GeminiApiService::class.java)

    }
```

```kotlin
}

fun bitmapToBase64(bitmap: Bitmap): String {

    val byteArrayOutputStream =
ByteArrayOutputStream()

    bitmap.compress(Bitmap.CompressFormat.JPEG,
100, byteArrayOutputStream)

    val byteArray =
byteArrayOutputStream.toByteArray()

    return Base64.encodeToString(byteArray,
Base64.DEFAULT)

}

//Example Usage:
```

```kotlin
// val bitmap =
BitmapFactory.decodeResource(resources,
R.drawable.my_image)


// val base64Image = bitmapToBase64(bitmap)


// val request =
GeminiRequest(listOf(Content(listOf(Part("Describe
this image and write a short poem about it."),
Part(inlineData = InlineData("image/jpeg",
base64Image))))))


// val call =
GeminiApi.retrofit.generateContent(request)


// call.enqueue(object :
retrofit2.Callback<GeminiResponse> {


//     override fun onResponse(call:
Call<GeminiResponse>, response:
retrofit2.Response<GeminiResponse>) {
```

```
//      //Handle response.

//    }

//    override fun onFailure(call:
Call<GeminiResponse>, t: Throwable) {

//      //Handle Failure.

//    }

// })
```

My Take:

I'm truly excited about the creative potential of Gemini's multimodal generation capabilities. It allows developers to build apps that can produce unique and engaging content, opening up new avenues for artistic expression and user interaction.

Key Considerations:

- Experiment with different prompt styles to explore Gemini's capabilities.
- Optimize image processing to minimize latency.
- Implement content filtering to ensure responsible use.
- Always refer to the most up to date Google developer documentation.

6.3 Prompt Engineering and Creative Applications

We're about to delve into the realm of prompt engineering, a crucial skill for harnessing the power of Gemini models. Effective prompts are the key to unlocking Gemini's creative potential and building innovative Android applications.

Prompt Engineering: The Art of Guiding AI

Prompt engineering involves crafting input prompts that guide AI models to generate desired outputs.

- **Clarity and Specificity:**
  - Clear and specific prompts lead to more accurate and relevant results.
  - Avoid ambiguity and provide detailed instructions.

- **Context and Background:**
  - Provide context and background information to help Gemini understand the desired output.
  - This is especially important for complex tasks.
- **Iteration and Refinement:**
  - Prompt engineering is an iterative process.
  - Experiment with different prompts and refine them based on the results.

Creative Applications with Gemini:

1. **Content Generation:**
   - Generate stories, poems, articles, and other forms of creative writing.
   - Use prompts to specify the style, tone, and subject matter.
   -
2. **Image Creation and Manipulation:**
   - Generate images from text descriptions.
   - Combine text and image inputs to create unique visual content.
3. **Interactive Storytelling:**
   - Create interactive stories where users can influence the narrative through their prompts.

○ This allows for personalized and engaging experiences.

4. **Personalized Content:**
   ○ Generate personalized content based on user preferences and data.
   ○ This can include personalized recommendations, summaries, and creative outputs.

5. **Educational Tools:**
   ○ Create educational tools that generate interactive lessons and explanations.
   ○ Use prompts to tailor the content to the user's learning style.

Practical Considerations:

- **Prompt Structuring:**
  ○ Structure prompts to include clear instructions, context, and examples.
  ○ Use delimiters or keywords to separate different parts of the prompt.

- **API Parameter Tuning:**
  ○ Experiment with API parameters, such as temperature and top-k, to control the creativity and diversity of the generated output.

- Always refer to the most up to date Google documentation for the most accurate information.

- **User Interface Design:**
  - Design user interfaces that facilitate prompt creation and provide clear feedback to the user.
  - Consider providing examples and templates to guide users.

- **Content Safety:**
  - Implement content filtering to ensure that the generated content is safe and appropriate.
  - Consider user reporting mechanisms.

- **Latency and Performance:**
  - Optimize your code to minimize latency and provide a smooth user experience.
  - Image generation and complex text generation can be computationally intensive.

Conceptual Code Example (Kotlin with Retrofit - Interactive Storytelling):

Kotlin

```
//Conceptual Example. Gemini api implementation
will change.
```

```kotlin
import retrofit2.Call

import retrofit2.Retrofit

import retrofit2.converter.gson.GsonConverterFactory

import retrofit2.http.Body

import retrofit2.http.Headers

import retrofit2.http.POST

interface GeminiApiService {

    @Headers("Content-Type: application/json")

    @POST("generateContent")

    fun generateContent(@Body request:
GeminiRequest): Call<GeminiResponse>
```

```kotlin
}

data class GeminiRequest(val contents:
List<Content>)

data class Content(val parts: List<Part>)

data class Part(val text: String)

data class GeminiResponse(val candidates:
List<Candidate>)

data class Candidate(val content: Content)

object GeminiApi {

    private const val BASE_URL =
"YOUR_GEMINI_API_URL" //Replace with the
Correct Gemini API URL.

    val retrofit: GeminiApiService by lazy {
```

```kotlin
            Retrofit.Builder()

                .baseUrl(BASE_URL)

        .addConverterFactory(GsonConverterFactory.create())

                .build()

            .create(GeminiApiService::class.java)

        }

    }


    fun generateStoryContinuation(storySoFar: String,
    userChoice: String, callback: (String?) -> Unit) {

        val prompt = "Continue the
    story:\n$storySoFar\nUser choice:
    $userChoice\nContinuation:"
```

```kotlin
    val request =
GeminiRequest(listOf(Content(listOf(Part(prompt)))))

    val call =
GeminiApi.retrofit.generateContent(request)

    call.enqueue(object :
retrofit2.Callback<GeminiResponse> {

        override fun onResponse(call:
Call<GeminiResponse>, response:
retrofit2.Response<GeminiResponse>) {

            val continuation =
response.body()?.candidates?.firstOrNull()?.content?.par
ts?.firstOrNull()?.text

            callback(continuation)

        }
```

```kotlin
                override fun onFailure(call:
Call<GeminiResponse>, t: Throwable) {


            callback(null)


        }



    })



    }



    //Example Usage:



    // generateStoryContinuation("Once upon a time...",
"The hero went into the forest.", { continuation ->


    //    if (continuation != null) {


    //        //Display continuation to the user.


    //    }
```

// })

My Take:

I'm fascinated by the creative potential of prompt engineering. It allows us to collaborate with AI models to generate unique and engaging content. By mastering this skill, we can build truly innovative Android applications.

Key Considerations:

- Experiment with different prompt styles to explore Gemini's capabilities.
- Design user interfaces that facilitate prompt creation.
- Implement content filtering to ensure responsible use.
- Always refer to the most up to date Google developer documentation.

6.4 Google AI Studio Workflow

We're about to delve into Google AI Studio, a platform that streamlines the process of experimenting with and prototyping generative AI models. It's an invaluable tool for rapid iteration and testing before integrating models into your Android applications.

Google AI Studio: Rapid Prototyping for Generative AI

Google AI Studio provides a user-friendly interface for interacting with Gemini and other generative AI models.

- **Interactive Prototyping:**
  - AI Studio allows you to quickly test prompts and explore model capabilities.
  - This eliminates the need to write extensive code for initial experimentation.
- **Multimodal Input and Output:**
  - AI Studio supports multimodal inputs, including text and images, mirroring Gemini's capabilities.
  - You can visualize generated images and text directly within the platform.
- **Simplified API Interaction:**
  - AI Studio simplifies the process of interacting with the Gemini API.
  - It handles API requests and responses, allowing you to focus on prompt engineering.
- **Code Generation:**
  - AI Studio can generate code snippets that you can directly integrate into your Android projects.

- This streamlines the transition from prototyping to development.

Workflow in Google AI Studio:

1. **Prompt Creation:**
   - Start by crafting your input prompts within the AI Studio interface.
   - Experiment with different prompt structures and content.

2. **Model Interaction:**
   - Select the desired Gemini model and configure the API parameters.
   - Send your prompts to the model and observe the generated outputs.

3. **Output Evaluation:**
   - Evaluate the generated text and images for accuracy and relevance.
   - Refine your prompts based on the evaluation results.

4. **Code Generation (Optional):**
   - Generate code snippets for API integration.
   - Copy and paste the code into your Android Studio project.

5. **Iteration and Refinement:**
   - Iterate on your prompts and model parameters until you achieve the desired output.
   - AI Studio facilitates rapid experimentation and refinement.

Practical Considerations:

- **Prompt Engineering:**
  - Use AI Studio to refine your prompt engineering skills.
  - Experiment with various prompt styles and structures.
- **Model Parameter Tuning:**
  - Explore the effects of different API parameters on the generated output.
  - Find the optimal settings for your application.
- **Data Handling:**
  - AI Studio simplifies the handling of image data and other multimodal inputs.
  - Use it to test different input formats and combinations.

- **Code Generation Limitations:**
  - The generated code snippets may require further customization and integration.
  - Use them as a starting point for your Android development.
- **API Usage:**
  - Be mindful of API usage limits and pricing.
  - Monitor your usage and optimize your prompts to reduce costs.

Conceptual Workflow Example:

1. **Create a prompt:**
   - In AI Studio, craft a prompt like: "Generate a short story about a robot that learns to paint."
2. **Interact with Gemini:**
   - Select the Gemini model and send the prompt.
3. **Evaluate the output:**
   - Read the generated story and assess its creativity and coherence.
4. **Refine the prompt:**

- Modify the prompt to specify the robot's personality or the style of painting.

5. **Generate code:**
   - Use AI Studio to generate code snippets for integrating the story generation into your Android app.

6. **Integrate into Android Studio:**
   - Copy and paste the code into your Android Studio project and adapt it as needed.

My Take:

I've found Google AI Studio to be an invaluable tool for quickly prototyping generative AI concepts. It allows for rapid iteration and experimentation, which is essential for building innovative and engaging Android applications. By using AI Studio, we can reduce development time and improve the quality of our AI-powered apps.

Key Considerations:

- Use AI Studio to refine your prompt engineering skills.
- Experiment with different model parameters.
- Use the generated code as a starting point for your Android development.

- Always refer to the most up to date Google developer documentation.

Chapter 7: Building Multimodal AI Applications

Get ready to level up your AI game! We're moving beyond single-modal applications and diving into the exciting world of multimodal AI. This chapter will guide you through combining text and image generation to create interactive and context-aware experiences.

7.1 Combining Text and Image Generation

We're about to delve into the realm of multimodal content creation, where text and images work together to create richer and more engaging experiences. This is where AI truly shine, enabling us to build apps that go beyond traditional text-based or image-based interactions.

The Power of Multimodal Content

Combining text and image generation allows us to create:

- **Visually Enhanced Stories:**
  - Generate stories with accompanying images that illustrate key scenes or characters.

- This creates a more immersive and engaging narrative.

- **Dynamic Product Descriptions:**
  - Generate product descriptions that include both textual details and visually appealing images.
  - This can improve product understanding and increase sales.

- **Personalized Content:**
  - Generate personalized content that combines user-provided text and images.
  - This can include personalized greetings, invitations, and creative outputs.

- **Interactive Educational Materials:**
  - Generate interactive educational materials that combine textual explanations with visual aids.
  - This can enhance learning and comprehension.

Practical Considerations:

1. **Data Synchronization:**
   - Ensure that the generated text and images are synchronized and coherent.
   - The text should accurately describe the image, and vice versa.

2. **Image Quality and Resolution:**
   - Optimize image quality and resolution for different screen sizes and devices.
   - Consider using vector graphics or scalable image formats.

3. **Text Formatting and Styling:**
   - Format and style the generated text to match the visual design of the app.
   - Consider using different fonts, colors, and layouts.

4. **User Interaction:**
   - Design user interfaces that allow users to interact with both the generated text and images.
   - Consider providing options for editing, sharing, and saving the content.

5. **Performance Optimization:**
   - Optimize image loading and processing to minimize latency.
   - Use asynchronous operations to avoid blocking the UI thread.

6. **API Integration:**
   - Understand the nuances of the API being used.

- Error handling, and data parsing are very important.

7. **Content Safety:**
    - Implement content filtering to ensure that the generated content is safe and appropriate.
    - Consider user reporting mechanisms.

Conceptual Code Example (Kotlin with Retrofit - Combined Text and Image Display):

Kotlin

```
//Conceptual Example. Gemini API
implementation will change.


import retrofit2.Call


import retrofit2.Retrofit


import
retrofit2.converter.gson.GsonConverterFactory
```

```
import retrofit2.http.Body


import retrofit2.http.Headers


import retrofit2.http.POST


import android.graphics.Bitmap


import android.graphics.BitmapFactory


import android.widget.ImageView


import android.widget.TextView


import java.io.ByteArrayInputStream


import android.util.Base64
```

```kotlin
interface GeminiApiService {

    @Headers("Content-Type: application/json")

    @POST("generateContent")

    fun generateContent(@Body request:
    GeminiRequest): Call<GeminiResponse>

}


data class GeminiRequest(val contents:
List<Content>)


data class Content(val parts: List<Part>)
```

```kotlin
data class Part(val text: String?, val inlineData:
InlineData?)


data class InlineData(val mimeType: String, val
data: String)


data class GeminiResponse(val candidates:
List<Candidate>)


data class Candidate(val content: Content)


object GeminiApi {


    private const val BASE_URL =
"YOUR_GEMINI_API_URL" //Replace with the
Correct Gemini API URL.
```

```kotlin
val retrofit: GeminiApiService by lazy {

    Retrofit.Builder()

        .baseUrl(BASE_URL)

        .addConverterFactory(GsonConverterFactory.create())

        .build()

        .create(GeminiApiService::class.java)

    }

}
```

```kotlin
fun displayGeneratedContent(textView:
TextView, imageView: ImageView, request:
GeminiRequest) {


    val call =
GeminiApi.retrofit.generateContent(request)


    call.enqueue(object :
retrofit2.Callback<GeminiResponse> {


override fun onResponse(call: Call<GeminiResponse>,
response: retrofit2.Response<GeminiResponse>) {


    val content =
response.body()?.candidates?.firstOrNull()?.content?.parts


    if (content != null) {


        for (part in content) {
```

```
if (part.text != null) {

    textView.text = part.text

}


if (part.inlineData != null &&
part.inlineData.mimeType == "image/jpeg") {

    val decodedBytes =
Base64.decode(part.inlineData.data, Base64.DEFAULT)


    val bitmap =
BitmapFactory.decodeStream(ByteArrayInputStream(decoded
Bytes))


    imageView.setImageBitmap(bitmap)
```

```
                    }



                }




            }




        }




        override fun onFailure(call: Call<GeminiResponse>, t:
Throwable) {



            //Handle Failure.



        }



    })
```

```
}


//Example Usage:


//val textView =
findViewById<TextView>(R.id.generatedText)


//val imageView =
findViewById<ImageView>(R.id.generatedImage)


//val request =
GeminiRequest(listOf(Content(listOf(Part("Generate a picture
of a cat, and write a poem about it.")))))


//displayGeneratedContent(textView, imageView, request)
```

My Take:

I'm truly excited about the potential of combining text and image generation. It allows us to build apps that are not only informative but also visually engaging. By mastering these techniques, we can create truly immersive and interactive Android experiences.

Key Considerations:

- Ensure data synchronization between text and images.
- Optimize image quality and resolution.
- Design user interfaces that facilitate interaction with both text and images.
- Implement robust error handling and content filtering.
- Always refer to the most up to date Google developer documentation.

7.2 Interactive and Context-Aware AI Experiences

We're about to delve into the realm of building AI experiences that are not only intelligent but also responsive and adaptive. This is where AI truly become a powerful tool for creating personalized and engaging interactions.

The Power of Interaction and Context

Building interactive and context-aware AI experiences allows us to create:

- **Personalized Recommendations:**
  - AI can analyze user interactions and context to provide tailored recommendations.
  - This can include product recommendations, content suggestions, and more.
    -

- **Adaptive User Interfaces:**
  - AI can adapt the user interface based on user behavior and context.
  - This can include adjusting layouts, displaying relevant information, and providing personalized assistance.

- **Contextual Assistance:**
  - AI can provide contextual assistance based on the user's current activity and environment.
  - This can include providing relevant information, suggesting actions, and answering questions.

- **Interactive Storytelling and Games:**
  - ○ AI can create interactive stories and games that adapt to user choices and actions.
  - ○ This allows for personalized and dynamic narratives.

Practical Considerations:

1. **Contextual Data Gathering:**
   - ○ Gather relevant contextual data, such as location, time, user activity, and device sensors.
   - ○ Respect user privacy and obtain explicit consent for data collection.

2. **User Interaction Tracking:**
   - ○ Track user interactions within the app, such as clicks, swipes, and text input.
   - ○ Analyze interaction patterns to understand user behavior.

3. **Contextual Reasoning:**
   - ○ Use AI models to reason about the user's context and interactions.
   - ○ This can involve natural language processing, machine learning, and rule-based systems.

4. **Dynamic Content Generation:**

- Generate dynamic content that adapts to the user's context and interactions.
- This can include personalized messages, recommendations, and creative outputs.

5. **Adaptive UI Design:**
   - Design user interfaces that can adapt to different contexts and user preferences.
   - Consider using responsive layouts and dynamic content placement.

6. **Real-Time Responsiveness:**
   - Ensure that the AI experience is responsive and provides real-time feedback.
   - Optimize code and models for low latency.

7. **Ethical Considerations:**
   - Address ethical concerns related to personalization and context awareness.
   - Ensure transparency and avoid discriminatory practices.

Conceptual Code Example (Kotlin - Context-Aware Recommendations):

Kotlin

```kotlin
import android.content.Context

import android.location.Location

import android.location.LocationManager

import kotlinx.coroutines.*

data class Recommendation(val title: String, val
description: String)

class ContextAwareRecommendations(private
val context: Context) {
```

```kotlin
private val locationManager =
context.getSystemService(Context.LOCATION_S
ERVICE) as LocationManager


@SuppressLint("MissingPermission")


fun getLocation(): Location? {


return try {


locationManager.getLastKnownLocation(Locatio
nManager.GPS_PROVIDER)


} catch (e: SecurityException) {


null
```

```kotlin
        }


    }


    suspend fun
getRecommendations(userPreferences:
Map<String, Any>): List<Recommendation> =
withContext(Dispatchers.IO) {


        val location = getLocation()


        val recommendations =
mutableListOf<Recommendation>()


        if (location != null) {


            // Example: Recommend nearby
restaurants based on location and user
preferences.
```

```
        // Replace with actual AI model or API
call.


        if (userPreferences["foodType"] ==
"Italian") {



recommendations.add(Recommendation("Italian
Restaurant A", "A great Italian restaurant near
you."))



recommendations.add(Recommendation("Italian
Restaurant B", "Another Italian option close by."))



        } else {



recommendations.add(Recommendation("Generic
Restaurant", "A restaurant near you."))
```

```
        }



    } else {



        // Example: Recommend general
content based on user preferences.



        // Replace with actual AI model or API
call.



    recommendations.add(Recommendation("General
Content 1", "Content you might enjoy."))



        recommendations.add(Recommendation("General
Content 2", "Another piece of content."))



        }
```

```
                    recommendations


          }


      }


      //Example Usage:


      //val recommendations =
ContextAwareRecommendations(this)


      //CoroutineScope(Dispatchers.Main).launch {


      //    val userPrefs = mapOf("foodType" to
"Italian")
```

```
//   val results =
recommendations.getRecommendations(userPrefs
)
```

```
//   //Display results to the user.
```

```
//}
```

My Take:

I'm fascinated by the potential of interactive and context-aware AI experiences. They allow us to build apps that feel truly personalized and responsive. By mastering these techniques, we can create Android applications that are not only intelligent but also intuitive and engaging.

Key Considerations:

- Prioritize user privacy and obtain explicit consent for data collection.
- Analyze user interactions to understand their behavior and preferences.

- Use AI models to reason about context and generate dynamic content.
- Design adaptive user interfaces that respond to different contexts.
- Implement real-time responsiveness and address ethical concerns.
- Always refer to the most up to date Google developer documentation.

7.3 Practical Multimodal App Development Examples

We're about to put our multimodal skills to the test by building some real-world application examples. Let's get started!

Example 1: AI-Powered Storybook Generator

This example demonstrates how to combine text and image generation to create interactive storybooks.

- **Functionality:**
  - Users provide a short prompt or theme.
  - The app generates a story and accompanying images.
  - Users can interact with the story and images.

- **Implementation (Conceptual):**

Kotlin

```
//Conceptual Example. Gemini api implementation will change.

import retrofit2.Call

import retrofit2.Retrofit

import retrofit2.converter.gson.GsonConverterFactory

import retrofit2.http.Body

import retrofit2.http.Headers

import retrofit2.http.POST

import android.graphics.Bitmap

import android.graphics.BitmapFactory

import android.widget.ImageView

import android.widget.TextView

import java.io.ByteArrayInputStream

import android.util.Base64
```

```kotlin
//... (Retrofit and data classes from previous examples)


class StorybookGenerator {


    fun generateStorybook(prompt: String, textView:
TextView, imageView: ImageView) {

        val storyPrompt = "Generate a short story based on the
theme: $prompt."

        val imagePrompt = "Generate an image that illustrates
a key scene from the story."


        val request = GeminiRequest(listOf(

            Content(listOf(Part(storyPrompt))),

            Content(listOf(Part(imagePrompt)))

        ))
```

```kotlin
val call = GeminiApi.retrofit.generateContent(request)

call.enqueue(object :
retrofit2.Callback<GeminiResponse> {

    override fun onResponse(call:
Call<GeminiResponse>, response:
retrofit2.Response<GeminiResponse>) {

        val content =
response.body()?.candidates?.firstOrNull()?.content?.parts

        if (content != null && content.size >= 2) {

            textView.text = content[0].text ?: "Story
generation failed."

            if (content[1].inlineData != null &&
content[1].inlineData?.mimeType == "image/jpeg") {

                val decodedBytes =
Base64.decode(content[1].inlineData?.data,
Base64.DEFAULT)

                val bitmap =
BitmapFactory.decodeStream(ByteArrayInputStream(decoded
Bytes))
```

```kotlin
                imageView.setImageBitmap(bitmap)

        } else {

            //Handle image generation failure.

            }

        } else {

            // Handle api failure.

            }

        }



        override fun onFailure(call: Call<GeminiResponse>,
t: Throwable) {

            //Handle Failure.

            }

        })

        }

    }
```

```kotlin
//Example usage:

// val generator = StorybookGenerator()

// generator.generateStorybook("A robot exploring a new
planet", storyTextView, storyImageView)
```

Example 2: AI-Powered Product Visualizer

This example demonstrates how to combine text and image generation to create dynamic product visualizations.

- **Functionality:**
    - Users provide a product description or specifications.
    - The app generates a visual representation of the product.
    - Users can interact with the visualization and modify the product.
- **Implementation (Conceptual):**

Kotlin

```kotlin
//Conceptual Example. Gemini API implementation will change.
```

```kotlin
//... (Retrofit and data classes from previous examples)


class ProductVisualizer {


    fun visualizeProduct(description: String, imageView:
ImageView) {

        val imagePrompt = "Generate an image of a product
based on the description: $description."


        val request =
GeminiRequest(listOf(Content(listOf(Part(imagePrompt)))))


        val call = GeminiApi.retrofit.generateContent(request)

        call.enqueue(object :
retrofit2.Callback<GeminiResponse> {

            override fun onResponse(call:
Call<GeminiResponse>, response:
retrofit2.Response<GeminiResponse>) {
```

```kotlin
        val content =
response.body()?.candidates?.firstOrNull()?.content?.parts

        if (content != null && content.isNotEmpty() &&
content[0].inlineData != null &&
content[0].inlineData?.mimeType == "image/jpeg") {

        val decodedBytes =
Base64.decode(content[0].inlineData?.data,
Base64.DEFAULT)

        val bitmap =
BitmapFactory.decodeStream(ByteArrayInputStream(decoded
Bytes))

        imageView.setImageBitmap(bitmap)

    } else {

    //Handle image generation failure.

    }

  }
```

```
        override fun onFailure(call: Call<GeminiResponse>,
t: Throwable) {

            //Handle Failure.

        }

    })

    }

}

//Example Usage:

// val visualizer = ProductVisualizer()

// visualizer.visualizeProduct("A futuristic electric car with a
sleek design", productImageView)
```

Example 3: AI-Powered Personalized Greeting Card Generator

- **Functionality:**
  - Users provide text and an image of a person.
  - The app will generate a personalized greeting card.

- **Implementation (Conceptual):**
  - Combine image and text data into the Gemini Api request.
  - Display the result to the user.

Key Considerations:

- **API Usage:**
  - Be mindful of API usage limits and pricing.
- **Performance:**
  - Optimize image loading and processing for smooth performance.
- **User Interface:**
  - Design intuitive user interfaces that facilitate interaction.
- **Error Handling:**
  - Implement robust error handling to manage API errors and other issues.
- **Content Safety:**
  - Implement content filtering to ensure responsible use.

My Take:

I'm excited about the possibilities of multimodal app development. By combining text and image generation, we can create truly unique and engaging experiences. These examples provide a starting point for your own creative explorations.

Chapter 8: Fine-Tuning and Model Adaptation

We've covered the basics of using pre-trained models. Now, let's explore how to customize them for our unique needs. Fine-tuning and adaptation are key to creating high-performance, specialized AI apps.

8.1 Transfer Learning for Android AI

We're about to delve into the world of transfer learning, a technique that allows us to leverage pre-trained models and adapt them to our specific tasks, saving us time and resources. Let's get started.

The Power of Transfer Learning

Transfer learning allows us to:

- **Reduce Training Time:**
    - Leverage pre-trained models that have already learned general features from large datasets.
    - This significantly reduces the amount of data and time required for training.
- **Improve Model Performance:**

- Benefit from the knowledge learned by pre-trained models.
- This can lead to better accuracy and generalization, especially with limited data.

- **Adapt to Specific Tasks:**
  - Fine-tune pre-trained models to adapt them to specific tasks and datasets.
  - This allows us to customize models for our Android application needs.

Key Concepts:

1. **Pre-trained Models:**
   - Models that have been trained on large datasets for general tasks, such as image classification or language modeling.
   - Examples: MobileNet, EfficientNet, BERT.

2. **Feature Extraction:**
   - Using the pre-trained model as a feature extractor.
   - Freeze the pre-trained layers and train only the new classification or regression layers.

3. **Fine-tuning:**
   - Unfreeze some or all of the pre-trained layers and train them along with the new layers.
   - This requires more data and computational resources.

Practical Implementation (Kotlin - Conceptual with TensorFlow Lite):

Kotlin

```
//Conceptual Example. TensorFlow Lite does not
perform training on device.


//Training must be done on a desktop environment,
and then the model can be used on device.


//Conceptual explanation of how the training process
would work.
```

//1. Load a pre-trained model using Tensorflow Keras on a desktop environment.

//2. Remove the final classification layers.

//3. Add new classification layers that match the target task.

//4. Freeze the pre-trained layers.

//5. Train the new layers with the specific dataset.

//6. (Optional) Unfreeze some of the pre-trained layers and fine-tune.

//7. Convert the trained model to TensorFlow Lite format.

//8. Load the TFLite model into the Android app.

//9. Run inference with the model.

```kotlin
//Example of loading a TFLite model on Android.

import android.content.res.AssetManager

import org.tensorflow.lite.Interpreter

import org.tensorflow.lite.support.common.FileUtil

import java.nio.MappedByteBuffer

class TransferLearningModel(assetManager:
AssetManager, modelFile: String) {

    private var interpreter: Interpreter? = null

    init {

        try {
```

```kotlin
        val model =
FileUtil.loadMappedFile(assetManager, modelFile)

        interpreter = Interpreter(model)

    } catch (e: Exception) {

        e.printStackTrace()

    }

}


    fun runInference(inputData: FloatArray,
outputBuffer: FloatArray) {

        interpreter?.run(inputData, outputBuffer)

    }

}
```

```
//Example Usage:


// val model = TransferLearningModel(assets,
"transfer_learned_model.tflite")


// model.runInference(inputData, outputBuffer)
```

Practical Considerations:

1. **Dataset Size:**
   - Fine-tuning requires a sufficient amount of data to avoid overfitting.
   - Feature extraction can be effective with smaller datasets.

2. **Computational Resources:**
   - Fine-tuning can be computationally intensive and may require powerful hardware.
   - Feature extraction is less demanding.

3. **Model Compatibility:**
   - Ensure that the pre-trained model is compatible with TensorFlow Lite.

- Some models may require conversion or optimization.

4. **Hardware Acceleration:**
   - Leverage GPUs and NPUs for faster inference.
   - As covered in chapter 2.3.

5. **Performance Optimization:**
   - Quantize and prune the model to reduce size and improve performance.
   - As covered in chapter 3.1.

6. **Data Preprocessing:**
   - Ensure that the input data is preprocessed in the same way as the data used to train the pre-trained model.

My Take:

I've found that transfer learning is a powerful tool for building AI-powered Android applications. It allows us to leverage the knowledge of pre-trained models and adapt them to our specific needs, saving us time and resources. By mastering these techniques, we can create more accurate and efficient AI experiences.

Key Considerations:

- Choose pre-trained models that are relevant to your task.
- Consider the trade-offs between feature extraction and fine-tuning.
- Optimize the model for on-device performance.
- Ensure data preprocessing consistency.
- Always refer to the most up to date Google developer documentation.

8.2 Adapting Pre-trained Models for Specific Tasks

We're diving into the art of tailoring pre-trained models to suit our specific needs. This is where the real power of transfer learning shines, allowing us to create highly customized AI experiences for Android.

The Necessity of Adaptation

Pre-trained models are powerful, but they are general-purpose. To make them truly effective for our Android apps, we need to adapt them to our specific tasks.

Key Adaptation Techniques:

1. **Feature Extraction (Simpler Adaptation):**
   - **Freezing Pre-trained Layers:**

- Keep the pre-trained layers frozen, preventing them from being updated during training.
- This preserves the general features learned by the model.

- **Adding New Layers:**
  - Add new, task-specific layers on top of the frozen layers.
  - These new layers will learn to map the pre-trained features to the target task.

- **Use Case:**
  - Useful when you have a small dataset or limited computational resources.

- **Conceptual Code (TensorFlow Keras, Desktop environment):**

Python

```
#Conceptual python example, done on a desktop.


import tensorflow as tf
```

```python
from tensorflow.keras.applications import MobileNetV2

from tensorflow.keras.layers import Dense, GlobalAveragePooling2D

from tensorflow.keras.models import Model

# Load a pre-trained MobileNetV2 model.

base_model = MobileNetV2(weights='imagenet', include_top=False, input_shape=(224, 224, 3))

# Freeze the pre-trained layers.

for layer in base_model.layers:

    layer.trainable = False
```

```python
# Add new classification layers.

x = base_model.output

x = GlobalAveragePooling2D()(x)

x = Dense(1024, activation='relu')(x)

predictions = Dense(10, activation='softmax')(x) # 10 classes

# Create the new model.

model = Model(inputs=base_model.input, outputs=predictions)

# Compile the model.

model.compile(optimizer='adam', loss='categorical_crossentropy', metrics=['accuracy'])
```

```
# Train the model.

# model.fit(...)

# Convert to TFLite and deploy to Android.

# converter =
tf.lite.TFLiteConverter.from_keras_model(model)

# tflite_model = converter.convert()

# open("converted_model.tflite",
"wb").write(tflite_model)
```

2. **Fine-tuning (More Complex Adaptation):**
   - ○ **Unfreezing Some Layers:**
     - ■ Unfreeze some of the top layers of the pre-trained model.
     - ■ This allows the model to adapt the pre-trained features to the specific task.

- Training with Specific Data:
    - Train the entire model (including the unfrozen layers) with the specific dataset.
- Use Case:
    - Useful when you have a larger dataset and more computational resources.
- Considerations:
    - Fine-tuning requires careful adjustment of learning rates and other training parameters.
    - Overfitting is a potential risk.

3. **Data Augmentation:**
    - **Enhancing Dataset Variability:**
        - Augment the training data with random transformations (rotations, flips, zooms).
        - This helps the model generalize better to unseen data.
    - **Conceptual Code (Tensorflow keras, desktop):**

Python

#Conceptual python example, done on a desktop.

```python
#... (Previous model setup)

from tensorflow.keras.preprocessing.image import
ImageDataGenerator

datagen = ImageDataGenerator(

    rotation_range=20,

    width_shift_range=0.2,

    height_shift_range=0.2,

    horizontal_flip=True

)
```

```
# Train the model with data augmentation.

# model.fit(datagen.flow(...))
```

Practical Considerations:

- **Dataset Size and Quality:**
  - The size and quality of your dataset are crucial for successful adaptation.
  - Ensure that your dataset is representative of the target task.
  -

- **Computational Resources:**
  - Fine-tuning can be computationally intensive.
  - Consider using cloud-based GPUs or TPUs for training.

- **Model Compatibility:**
  - Ensure that the pre-trained model is compatible with TensorFlow Lite.
  - Some models may require conversion or optimization.

- **Performance Optimization:**
  - Quantize and prune the adapted model for on-device performance.
  - As covered in chapter 3.1.
- **Data Preprocessing:**
  - Maintain consistent data preprocessing between training and inference.

My Take:

I've found that adapting pre-trained models is a powerful way to create highly customized AI experiences for Android. By carefully selecting and adapting pre-trained models, we can significantly reduce development time and improve model performance.

Key Considerations:

- Choose the appropriate adaptation technique (feature extraction or fine-tuning).
- Ensure that your dataset is representative and of sufficient size.
- Optimize the model for on-device performance.
- Maintain consistent data preprocessing.

- Always refer to the most up to date Google developer documentation.

By understanding the fundamentals of adapting pre-trained models for specific tasks, you can begin to explore the possibilities of building truly customized AI experiences for Android.

8.3 Performance Optimization and Customization

We're about to fine-tune our adapted models for optimal performance on Android devices. This involves a combination of optimization techniques and customization strategies.

The Necessity of Optimization and Customization

Android devices have limited resources, so we need to optimize our models for speed and efficiency. Customization ensures that our models are tailored to the specific needs of our applications.

Key Optimization and Customization Techniques:

1. **Model Quantization (Recap):**
   - **Reducing Model Size and Inference Time:**

- Convert model weights and activations from floating-point to integer representations.
- This reduces model size and speeds up inference.

- **Post-Training Quantization:**
  - Quantize the model after training.
  - As covered in chapter 3.1.

- **Quantization-Aware Training:**
  - Train the model with quantization in mind.
  - This can lead to better accuracy compared to post-training quantization.

- **TensorFlow Lite Support:**
  - TensorFlow Lite has built in quantization support.

2. **Model Pruning (Recap):**

- **Reducing Model Complexity:**
  - Remove unnecessary connections (weights) from the model.
  - This reduces model size and computational requirements.

- **TensorFlow Model Optimization Toolkit:**

- Provides tools for pruning models during training.
- As covered in chapter 3.1.

3. **Hardware Acceleration (Recap):**

   o **Leveraging GPUs and NPUs:**

   - Use TensorFlow Lite delegates to enable GPU and NPU acceleration.
   - This significantly speeds up inference.
   - As covered in chapter 2.3.

4. **Custom Operations (Advanced Customization):**

   o **Implementing Specialized Operations:**

   - Create custom TensorFlow Lite operations for specific tasks.
   - This allows you to optimize performance for unique computations.

   o **Use Case:**

   - Useful when standard TensorFlow Lite operations are not efficient enough.

   o **Considerations:**

   - Requires knowledge of TensorFlow Lite internals and C++ programming.
   - Complex to implement and maintain.

5. **Model Architecture Optimization:**

- Selecting Efficient Architectures:
    - Choose model architectures that are optimized for mobile devices.
    - Examples: MobileNet, EfficientNet, MobileBERT.
- Architecture Modification:
    - Modify the model architecture to reduce complexity and improve performance.
    - This may involve removing layers or reducing the number of parameters.
-
- Considerations:
    - Requires a deep understanding of model architectures.
    - May require retraining the model.

6. Data Preprocessing Optimization:
    - Efficient Data Handling:
        - Optimize data preprocessing steps to reduce latency.
        - Avoid unnecessary computations and memory allocations.
    - Asynchronous Preprocessing:

- Perform data preprocessing on a background thread.
- This prevents blocking the UI thread.
  - **Example:**
    - Use efficient image resizing algorithms.

Practical Considerations:

- **Accuracy Trade-offs:**
  - Optimization techniques can sometimes reduce model accuracy.
  - Experiment with different techniques and parameters to find the best balance.
- **Hardware Compatibility:**
  - Ensure that the optimized model is compatible with the target Android devices.
  - Test your model on a variety of devices.
- **Profiling and Benchmarking:**
  - Use profiling tools to identify performance bottlenecks.
  - Use benchmarking tools to measure model performance.

- Tensorflow lite benchmark tool, and Android studio profiler are very useful.
- **Iterative Optimization:**
  - Optimization is an iterative process.
  - Continuously refine your model and code based on performance measurements.

My Take:

I've found that performance optimization and customization are essential for building successful AI-powered Android applications. By carefully applying these techniques, we can create models that are both efficient and tailored to our specific needs.

Key Considerations:

- Quantize and prune your model for on-device performance.
- Leverage hardware acceleration (GPUs and NPUs).
- Consider custom operations for specialized tasks.
- Optimize the model architecture and data preprocessing.
- Profile and benchmark your model to identify bottlenecks.

- Always refer to the most up to date Google developer documentation.

Chapter 9: Deployment and Performance Optimization

We've built some amazing AI models, but now it's time to get them into the hands of users. This chapter will guide you through the crucial steps of deploying and optimizing your models for Android. Let's make sure our apps perform at their best!

9.1 Profiling and Optimizing AI Models for Android

We've adapted and customized our models, but now it's time to ensure they perform optimally on Android. Profiling and optimization are crucial steps in this process.

The Importance of Profiling and Optimization

Android devices have limited resources, so we need to profile our models to identify bottlenecks and optimize them for speed and efficiency.

Key Profiling Techniques:

1. **TensorFlow Lite Profiler:**
    - **Identifying Performance Bottlenecks:**

- The TensorFlow Lite profiler provides detailed information about the execution time of different operations in your model.
- This helps identify areas where optimization is needed.

○ **Usage:**

- Enable profiling in the TensorFlow Lite interpreter options.
- Use the profiler's output to analyze performance.

○ **Conceptual Code (Kotlin):**

Kotlin

```kotlin
import org.tensorflow.lite.Interpreter

import org.tensorflow.lite.Interpreter.Options



fun runInferenceWithProfiling(interpreter: Interpreter,
inputData: FloatArray, outputBuffer: FloatArray) {

    val options = Options()

    options.setEnableProfiling(true)
```

```kotlin
    val profiledInterpreter = Interpreter(interpreter.model,
options)

    profiledInterpreter.run(inputData, outputBuffer)

    val profileData = profiledInterpreter.getProfiler().export()

    // Process the profileData (e.g., log it or display it).

    println(profileData)


    profiledInterpreter.close()

}
```

2. **Android Studio Profiler:**
    o **Monitoring CPU and Memory Usage:**
        ▪ The Android Studio profiler provides real-time information about CPU and memory usage.
        ▪ This helps identify resource-intensive operations.

- Usage:
    - Use the Android Studio profiler to monitor your app's performance while running inference.
    - Analyze the CPU and memory graphs to identify spikes and bottlenecks.

3. **TensorFlow Lite Benchmark Tool:**
    - **Measuring Inference Latency:**
        - The TensorFlow Lite benchmark tool measures the inference latency of your model on different Android devices.
        - This helps evaluate the model's performance in real-world scenarios.
    - **Usage:**
        - Use the benchmark tool to run inference on your model and collect performance metrics.
        - Analyze the results to identify areas for optimization.

Key Optimization Techniques (Recap and Expansion):

1. **Model Quantization and Pruning:**
   - **Reducing Model Size and Complexity:**
     - As covered in chapter 8.3, these techniques reduce model size and improve inference speed.

2. **Hardware Acceleration (GPUs and NPUs):**
   - **Leveraging Device Hardware:**
     - As covered in chapter 8.3, use TensorFlow Lite delegates for hardware acceleration.

3. **Efficient Data Preprocessing:**
   - **Minimizing Preprocessing Overhead:**
     - Optimize data preprocessing steps to reduce latency.
     - Use efficient algorithms and avoid unnecessary computations.
   - **Asynchronous Preprocessing:**
     - Perform preprocessing on a background thread.
     - This prevents blocking the UI thread.

4. **Model Architecture Optimization (Recap):**
   - **Selecting Efficient Architectures:**

- As covered in chapter 8.3, choose architectures optimized for mobile.

5. **Thread Management:**
   - **Asynchronous Inference:**
     - Run inference on a background thread to avoid blocking the UI thread.
     - As covered in chapter 3.2.
   - **Thread Pooling:**
     - Use thread pools to manage multiple inference requests efficiently.

Practical Considerations:

- **Device Variations:**
  - Performance can vary across different Android devices.
  - Test your model on a variety of devices.
- **Accuracy Trade-offs:**
  - Optimization techniques can sometimes reduce model accuracy.
  - Find the best balance between performance and accuracy.
  -

- **Iterative Optimization:**
  - Optimization is an iterative process.
  - Continuously refine your model and code based on profiling results.
- **Power Consumption:**
  - High-performance inference can consume significant power.
  - Optimize your model and code to conserve battery life.

My Take:

I've found that profiling and optimization are essential for building high-performing AI-powered Android applications. By carefully analyzing performance bottlenecks and applying optimization techniques, we can create smooth and efficient user experiences.

Key Considerations:

- Use the TensorFlow Lite profiler, Android Studio profiler, and benchmark tool to identify bottlenecks.
- Apply quantization, pruning, and hardware acceleration techniques.
- Optimize data preprocessing and model architecture.

- Manage threads efficiently.

- Test your model on a variety of devices.

- Always refer to the most up to date Google developer documentation.

9.2 Deploying Models to Google Play Store

We've built, optimized, and tested our AI-powered Android app. Now, it's time to share it with the world. Let's walk through the deployment process to the Google Play Store.

Preparing Your App for Deployment:

1. **Thorough Testing:**
   - **Device Compatibility:**
     - Test your app on a variety of Android devices with different hardware configurations.
     - Ensure your AI models perform well across different devices.
   - **Performance Testing:**
     - Use the techniques covered in chapter 9.1 to profile and benchmark your app's performance.
     - Optimize for speed and efficiency.

- o **User Testing:**
  - Conduct user testing to gather feedback and identify potential issues.
  - This helps improve the user experience.

2. **App Bundling:**
   - o **Android App Bundle (AAB):**
     - Use the Android App Bundle format for efficient app delivery.
     - AAB allows Google Play to deliver optimized APKs to users based on their device configurations.
   - o **Benefits:**
     - Reduced app size.
     - Improved download speeds.
     - Support for dynamic feature delivery.
   - o **Android Studio:**
     - Android studio makes it very easy to generate an AAB.

3. **Model Packaging:**
   - o **Asset Management:**
     - Include your TensorFlow Lite or other model files as assets in your app.

- Ensure that the models are properly packaged and accessible.
- **Dynamic Downloads (Optional):**
  - For large models, consider downloading them dynamically after app installation.
  - This reduces the initial app size.
- **Security:**
  - Do not include sensitive data inside your models.
  - Consider model encryption when necessary.

4. **Google Play Console Setup:**
   - **Developer Account:**
     - Create a Google Play Developer account.
   - **App Listing:**
     - Create a new app listing in the Google Play Console.
     - Provide detailed information about your app, including screenshots, descriptions, and privacy policies.
   - **App Releases:**
     - Create a new release for your app.
     - Upload your AAB file and provide release notes.

Deployment Process:

1. **Signing Your App:**
   - **App Signing Key:**
     - Sign your app with a release signing key.
     - This ensures that your app is authentic and cannot be tampered with.
   - **Google Play App Signing:**
     - Consider using Google Play App Signing for enhanced security.
     - Google manages your signing key and signs your app for distribution.[4]

2. **Uploading to Google Play Console:**
   - **Release Management:**
     - Navigate to the release management section in the Google Play Console.
     - Create a new release and upload your signed AAB file.

3. **Release Tracks:**
   - **Internal Testing:**
     - Use the internal testing track to test your app with a small group of trusted testers.
   - **Closed Testing:**

- Use the closed testing track to test your app with a larger group of testers.
  - ○ **Open Testing:**
    - Use the open testing track to test your app with a public audience.
  - ○ **Production Release:**
    - Use the production release track to release your app to the general public.
4. **Review and Publishing:**
   - ○ **Google Play Review:**
     - Google Play will review your app for compliance with policies.
     - This process can take several days.
   - ○ **Publishing:**
     - Once your app is approved, you can publish it to the Google Play Store.

Practical Considerations:

- **Privacy and Security:**
  - ○ Ensure that your app complies with all relevant privacy and security regulations.

- Clearly communicate your data collection and usage practices in your privacy policy.

- **User Feedback:**
  - Monitor user reviews and feedback after publishing your app.
  - Address user concerns and provide updates as needed.

- **App Updates:**
  - Plan for regular app updates to improve performance, add new features, and address bugs.
  - Use the Google Play Console to manage app updates.

- **A/B Testing:**
  - Use the Google Play Console to run A/B tests on your app listing and features.
  - This helps optimize your app for better performance.

My Take:

I've found that deploying to the Google Play Store requires careful planning and attention to detail. By following these steps, you can ensure that your AI-powered Android app reaches its intended audience and provides a positive user experience.

Key Considerations:

- Thoroughly test your app on a variety of devices.
- Use the Android App Bundle format for efficient delivery.
- Properly package and secure your AI models.
- Use the Google Play Console to manage your app releases.
- Monitor user feedback and provide regular updates.
- Always refer to the most up to date Google developer documentation.

9.3 Model Updates and Version Management

We've successfully deployed our AI-powered Android app, but our journey doesn't end there. Models evolve, bugs appear, and new features emerge. That's where model updates and version management come into play.

The Necessity of Model Updates and Version Management

AI models are not static. We need to update them for:

- **Improved Accuracy:**

- Models can be retrained with new data to improve accuracy.

- **Bug Fixes:**
  - Model updates can address bugs or performance issues.

- **New Features:**
  - New model versions can introduce new features or capabilities.

- **Security Updates:**
  - Model updates can address security vulnerabilities.

Key Techniques for Model Updates and Version Management:

1. **Dynamic Model Downloads:**
   - **Downloading Models at Runtime:**
     - Instead of bundling models with the app, download them dynamically from a remote server.
     - This allows you to update models without requiring users to update the entire app.
   - **Benefits:**
     - Reduced app size.

- Faster model updates.
- Flexibility in model management.
  - **Implementation (Kotlin - Conceptual):**

Kotlin

```kotlin
import kotlinx.coroutines.*

import java.io.File

import java.io.FileOutputStream

import java.net.URL


suspend fun downloadModel(modelUrl: String, destinationFile: File) {

    withContext(Dispatchers.IO) {

        try {

            val url = URL(modelUrl)

            val connection = url.openConnection()

            connection.connect()
```

```
        val inputStream = connection.getInputStream()

        val outputStream =
FileOutputStream(destinationFile)

        inputStream.copyTo(outputStream)

        inputStream.close()

        outputStream.close()

    } catch (e: Exception) {

        //Handle download failure.

        e.printStackTrace()

    }

  }

}


//Example Usage:
```

```
//val modelUrl =
"https://your-server.com/models/model_v2.tflite"

//val destinationFile = File(context.filesDir, "model.tflite")

//CoroutineScope(Dispatchers.Main).launch {

//   downloadModel(modelUrl, destinationFile)

//}
```

2. **Version Control:**
   - **Model Versioning:**
     - Assign version numbers to your models.
     - This helps track model changes and manage updates.
   - **Server-Side Management:**
     - Store model versions on a server and provide an API for version checking.
     - This allows your app to check for updates and download the latest version.
   - **Metadata:**
     - Store metadata along with the models, such as creation date, training data, and performance metrics.
3. **A/B Testing:**

- Testing Model Variations:
  - Deploy different model versions to different user groups.
  - This allows you to test the performance of new models before releasing them to all users.
- Remote Configuration:
  - Use remote configuration services (e.g., Firebase Remote Config) to manage A/B tests.
  - This allows you to control which model version is served to each user group.

4. Fallback Mechanisms:
  - Handling Download Failures:
    - Implement fallback mechanisms to handle model download failures.
    - This can include using a bundled model or displaying an error message.
  - Model Compatibility Checks:
    - Implement checks to ensure that the downloaded model is compatible with the device.

- This can prevent app crashes or unexpected behavior.

5. **Security Considerations:**
    - **Model Integrity:**
        - Verify the integrity of downloaded models to prevent tampering.
        - Use checksums or digital signatures.
    - **Secure Communication:**
        - Use HTTPS for secure model downloads.
        - This protects the models from interception.

Practical Considerations:

- **Bandwidth Usage:**
    - Be mindful of bandwidth usage when downloading models.
    - Consider using compression techniques.
- **Storage Space:**
    - Manage storage space efficiently to accommodate model updates.
    - Delete old model versions when they are no longer needed.
- **User Experience:**

- ○ Provide clear feedback to the user during model downloads and updates.
- ○ Avoid interrupting the user's workflow.

My Take:

I've found that model updates and version management are crucial for maintaining and improving AI-powered Android applications. By implementing these techniques, we can ensure that our apps remain up-to-date and provide a positive user experience.

Key Considerations:

- Use dynamic model downloads for flexibility.
- Implement version control for tracking model changes.
- Use A/B testing to evaluate new models.
- Implement fallback mechanisms for download failures.
- Prioritize security and user experience.
- Always refer to the most up to date Google developer documentation.

Chapter 10: Privacy and Security in Android AI

We've built some powerful AI apps, but with great power comes great responsibility. This chapter focuses on the ethical and practical aspects of privacy and security in Android AI development. Let's make sure we're building apps that users can trust.

10.1 Federated Learning and Privacy-Preserving Techniques

We're about to delve into the world of federated learning, a powerful approach that enables us to train AI models without compromising user privacy. Let's get started.

The Importance of Privacy in AI

Traditional machine learning often requires centralizing user data, which raises privacy concerns. Federated learning offers a solution by training models on decentralized data, keeping user data on their devices.

Federated Learning: Training Without Centralization

Federated learning involves:

- **Decentralized Training:**
  - Training AI models on user devices without sending raw data to a central server.
  - Only model updates are shared, not the data itself.
- **Local Model Updates:**
  - Each device trains a local model on its own data.
  - The device then sends the model updates (gradients) to a central server.
- **Aggregation:**
  - The central server aggregates the model updates from multiple devices.
  - This aggregated update is used to improve the global model.
- **Global Model Distribution:**
  - The improved global model is then distributed back to the devices.

Privacy-Preserving Techniques:

1. **Differential Privacy:**
   - **Adding Noise:**

- Adding carefully calibrated noise to the model updates before sending them to the server.
- This protects the privacy of individual data points.
  - **Benefits:**
    - Provides mathematical guarantees of privacy.
    - Limits the impact of individual data points on the model.

2. **Secure Aggregation:**
   - **Encrypting Model Updates:**
     - Encrypting model updates before sending them to the server.
     - The server can only aggregate the encrypted updates, not decrypt them.
   - **Benefits:**
     - Protects model updates from eavesdropping.
     - Ensures that the server cannot access individual updates.

3. **Homomorphic Encryption:**
   - **Performing Computations on Encrypted Data:**

- Allows computations to be performed on encrypted data without decrypting it.
- This enables secure aggregation and other privacy-preserving operations.
- **Benefits:**
  - Provides strong privacy guarantees.
  - Enables complex computations on encrypted data.

Practical Considerations:

1. **Communication Overhead:**
   - Federated learning involves frequent communication between devices and the server.
   - Optimize communication protocols to minimize overhead.
   -

2. **Device Heterogeneity:**
   - Android devices have varying processing power and network connectivity.
   - Design algorithms that can handle device heterogeneity.

3. **Data Heterogeneity:**

- User data can vary significantly across devices.
- Design algorithms that can handle data heterogeneity.

4. **Security:**
   - Implement robust security measures to protect model updates and data.
   - Use secure communication protocols and encryption techniques.

5. **Computational Resources:**
   - Training models on devices can be computationally intensive.
   - Optimize models for on-device performance.

Conceptual Code (Kotlin - Federated Learning Communication):

Kotlin

```kotlin
import kotlinx.coroutines.*

import java.net.HttpURLConnection

import java.net.URL

import java.io.OutputStreamWriter
```

```kotlin
import org.json.JSONObject


suspend fun sendModelUpdates(modelUpdates:
JSONObject, serverUrl: String) {

    withContext(Dispatchers.IO) {

        try {

            val url = URL(serverUrl)

            val connection = url.openConnection() as
HttpURLConnection

            connection.requestMethod = "POST"

            connection.setRequestProperty("Content-Type",
"application/json")

            connection.doOutput = true


            val outputStreamWriter =
OutputStreamWriter(connection.outputStream)

            outputStreamWriter.write(modelUpdates.toString())
```

```kotlin
            outputStreamWriter.flush()

            outputStreamWriter.close()


            val responseCode = connection.responseCode

            if (responseCode ==
HttpURLConnection.HTTP_OK) {

                // Handle successful response.

            } else {

                // Handle error.

            }

        } catch (e: Exception) {

            //Handle network error.

            e.printStackTrace()

        }

    }

}
```

```
//Example Usage:

//val modelUpdates = JSONObject().apply {

//    put("gradient_1", "value_1")

//    put("gradient_2", "value_2")

//}

//val serverUrl = "https://your-server.com/aggregate"

//CoroutineScope(Dispatchers.Main).launch {

//    sendModelUpdates(modelUpdates, serverUrl)

//}
```

My Take:

I've found that federated learning and privacy-preserving techniques are essential for building ethical and user-friendly AI applications. By prioritizing user privacy, we can foster trust and create AI experiences that are both powerful and responsible.

Key Considerations:

- Prioritize user privacy and data security.
- Optimize communication protocols for efficiency.
- Design algorithms that can handle device and data heterogeneity.
- Implement robust security measures.
- Consider the computational resources of Android devices.
- Always refer to the most up to date Google developer documentation.

10.2 Data Security and User Privacy Considerations

We're about to delve into the ethical and legal aspects of AI development, focusing on data security and user privacy. It's crucial to build AI applications that respect user rights and protect sensitive information.

The Foundation of Trust: Data Security and Privacy

Building user trust is essential for the success of any AI application. This trust is built upon a foundation of robust data security and respect for user privacy.

Key Considerations:

1. **Data Minimization:**
   - **Collecting Only Necessary Data:**
     - Only collect the data that is absolutely necessary for your application's functionality.
     - Avoid collecting sensitive or unnecessary information.
   - **Benefits:**
     - Reduces the risk of data breaches.
     - Minimizes the impact of potential privacy violations.

2. **Data Anonymization and Pseudonymization:**
   - **Removing Identifying Information:**
     - Anonymize or pseudonymize user data to remove or obscure personally identifiable information (PII).
     - This helps protect user privacy while still allowing for data analysis.
   - **Techniques:**
     - Data masking, tokenization, and generalization.

3. **Secure Data Storage:**

   - **Encrypting Data at Rest:**

     - Encrypt user data when it is stored on the device or in the cloud.
     - This prevents unauthorized access to sensitive information.

   - **Using Secure Storage Solutions:**

     - Use secure storage solutions provided by the Android platform or reputable cloud providers.
     - Avoid storing sensitive data in plain text.

4. **Secure Data Transmission:**

   - **Using HTTPS:**

     - Use HTTPS for all communication between your app and the server.
     - This encrypts data in transit and prevents eavesdropping.

   - **Secure APIs:**

     - Use secure APIs that implement authentication and authorization mechanisms.
     - This protects your app from unauthorized access.

5. **User Consent and Transparency:**
   - **Obtaining Explicit Consent:**
     - Obtain explicit user consent before collecting or using their data.
     - Provide clear and concise information about how their data will be used.
   - **Providing Transparent Privacy Policies:**
     - Create clear and easy-to-understand privacy policies.
     - Explain your data collection and usage practices in detail.

6. **Data Retention Policies:**
   - **Defining Data Retention Periods:**
     - Define clear data retention periods and delete data when it is no longer needed.
     - Avoid storing user data indefinitely.
   - **Implementing Data Deletion Mechanisms:**
     - Provide users with mechanisms to delete their data.
     - Respect user requests for data deletion.

7. **Compliance with Regulations:**

   o **GDPR, CCPA, and Other Regulations:**

      ■ Ensure that your app complies with all
        relevant data privacy regulations, such as
        GDPR and CCPA.

      ■ Stay up-to-date with evolving regulations.

8. **On-Device Processing:**

   o **Minimizing Data Transfer:**

      ■ Perform as much data processing as
        possible on the device.

      ■ This reduces the amount of data that needs
        to be transmitted to the server.

   o **TensorFlow Lite:**

      ■ TensorFlow lite allows for on-device
        processing.

Conceptual Code (Kotlin - Encrypted Shared Preferences):

Kotlin

```
import android.content.Context
```

```kotlin
import
androidx.security.crypto.EncryptedSharedPreferences

import androidx.security.crypto.MasterKeys

fun getEncryptedSharedPreferences(context:
Context): android.content.SharedPreferences {

    val masterKeyAlias =
MasterKeys.getOrCreate(MasterKeys.AES256_GCM_S
PEC)

    return EncryptedSharedPreferences.create(

        "secret_shared_prefs",

        masterKeyAlias,

        context,
```

```
EncryptedSharedPreferences.PrefKeyEncryptionScheme
.AES256_SIV,


EncryptedSharedPreferences.PrefValueEncryptionSche
me.AES256_GCM


    )


    }


    //Example Usage:


    //val sharedPreferences =
getEncryptedSharedPreferences(this)


    //sharedPreferences.edit().putString("sensitive_data",
"my_secret_value").apply()
```

My Take:

I've found that prioritizing data security and user privacy is not only an ethical imperative but also a crucial business strategy. By building trustworthy and responsible AI applications, we can foster user confidence and create a sustainable ecosystem.

Key Considerations:

- Implement data minimization and anonymization techniques.
- Use secure data storage and transmission methods.
- Obtain explicit user consent and provide transparent privacy policies.
- Define clear data retention policies and implement deletion mechanisms.
- Ensure compliance with relevant data privacy regulations.
- Perform on-device processing whenever possible.
- Always refer to the most up to date Google developer documentation and legal resources.

10.3 Best Practices for Secure AI Development

We're about to synthesize the essential principles of secure AI development, creating a robust framework for building responsible and reliable AI applications on Android.

Building a Secure AI Foundation:

Secure AI development is not an afterthought; it's a fundamental principle that should guide every stage of the development process.

Key Best Practices:

1. **Threat Modeling and Risk Assessment:**
   - **Identifying Potential Threats:**
     - Conduct a thorough threat modeling exercise to identify potential security risks and vulnerabilities.
     - Consider threats such as data breaches, model tampering, and adversarial attacks.
   - **Assessing Risk:**
     - Assess the potential impact of each threat and prioritize mitigation efforts.
   - **Tools:**

- Use threat modeling frameworks and tools to guide the process.

2. **Secure Model Development:**
   - **Adversarial Robustness:**
     - Train models to be robust against adversarial attacks, such as input manipulation.
     - Use techniques like adversarial training and input validation.
   - **Model Integrity:**
     - Implement mechanisms to verify the integrity of your models.
     - Use checksums or digital signatures to detect tampering.
   - **Secure Model Storage:**
     - Store models securely on the device or in the cloud.
     - Encrypt models when necessary.

3. **Secure Data Handling (Recap):**
   - **Data Minimization and Anonymization:**
     - As discussed in 10.2, collect only necessary data and anonymize or pseudonymize sensitive information.

- ○ **Secure Storage and Transmission:**
    - ■ As discussed in 10.2, encrypt data at rest and in transit.
- ○ **Data Validation:**
    - ■ Validate user input and data from external sources to prevent injection attacks and other vulnerabilities.

4. **Secure Communication (Recap):**
   - ○ **HTTPS and Secure APIs:**
       - ■ As discussed in 10.2, use HTTPS for all communication and secure APIs for data exchange.
   - ○ **Authentication and Authorization:**
       - ■ Implement robust authentication and authorization mechanisms to control access to your[1] app and data.

5. **Secure On-Device Processing:**
   - ○ **Minimizing Data Transfer:**
       - ■ Perform as much data processing as possible on the device to reduce the risk of data breaches.
   - ○ **Trusted Execution Environments (TEEs):**

- Leverage TEEs to isolate sensitive computations and data.
- This provides an extra layer of security.

6. **Regular Security Audits and Penetration Testing:**
   - **Identifying Vulnerabilities:**
     - Conduct regular security audits and penetration testing to identify vulnerabilities.
     - Engage third-party security experts for independent assessments.
   - **Continuous Monitoring:**
     - Implement continuous monitoring to detect and respond to security incidents.

7. **Software Updates and Patch Management:**
   - **Keeping Software Up-to-Date:**
     - Keep your app, libraries, and dependencies up-to-date with the latest security patches.
     - This prevents exploitation of known vulnerabilities.
   - **Over-the-Air (OTA) Updates:**
     - Implement OTA updates to deliver security patches and bug fixes to users quickly.

8. **User Education and Awareness:**

- o **Educating Users about Security Best Practices:**
  - Educate users about security best practices, such as strong passwords and avoiding phishing scams.
  - Provide clear and concise information about your app's security features.
- o **Transparency:**
  - Be transparent about your security practices and data handling procedures.

Conceptual Code (Kotlin - Input Validation):

Kotlin

```kotlin
fun validateInput(input: String): Boolean {

    // Implement input validation logic.

    // Example: Check for SQL injection characters.

    val sqlInjectionChars = arrayOf("'", ";", "--", "/*")

    for (char in sqlInjectionChars) {

        if (input.contains(char)) {
```

```
        return false

    }

  }

  // Add more validation rules as needed.

  return true

}

//Example Usage:

//val userInput = editText.text.toString()

//if (validateInput(userInput)) {

//   // Process the input.

//} else {

//   // Display an error message.

//}
```

My Take:

I've found that secure AI development is a continuous process
that requires vigilance and a proactive approach. By

implementing these best practices, we can build AI applications that are not only powerful but also inherently secure and trustworthy.

Key Considerations:

- Conduct thorough threat modeling and risk assessments.
- Develop models with adversarial robustness and integrity.
- Implement secure data handling and communication practices.
- Leverage secure on-device processing.
- Conduct regular security audits and penetration testing.
- Keep software up-to-date and educate users about security.
- Always refer to the most up to date Google developer documentation and security resources.

Chapter 11: The Future of Android AI

We've covered a lot of ground in this book, but the world of AI is constantly evolving. In this final chapter, we'll discuss the emerging trends and technologies that will shape the future of Android AI. Let's get ready for what's next

11.1 Emerging Trends and Technologies

We're about to embark on a journey into the future of Android AI. The field is constantly evolving, with new trends and technologies emerging at an incredible pace. Let's explore some of the most promising developments.

The Future of Android AI: A Glimpse into Tomorrow

1. **TinyML (Tiny Machine Learning):**
   - **Running AI on Microcontrollers:**
     - TinyML enables machine learning on resource-constrained devices like microcontrollers.
     - This opens up possibilities for AI in IoT devices, wearables, and other embedded systems.
   - **Benefits:**

- Low power consumption.
- Reduced latency.
- Enhanced privacy.
- **TensorFlow Lite Micro:**
  - TensorFlow Lite Micro is a version of TensorFlow Lite designed for microcontrollers.

2. **Edge AI:**
   - **Processing AI on the Edge:**
     - Edge AI involves processing AI models on edge devices (like smartphones) rather than in the cloud.
     - This reduces latency, conserves bandwidth, and enhances privacy.
   - **Benefits:**
     - Faster response times.
     - Offline functionality.
     - Enhanced data privacy.
   - **TensorFlow Lite:**
     - TensorFlow lite plays a large role in Edge AI on Android.

3. **Neural Architecture Search (NAS):**
   - **Automating Model Design:**

- NAS automates the process of designing neural network architectures.
- This allows developers to create highly optimized models for specific tasks and devices.

- **Benefits:**
  - Improved model performance.
  - Reduced development time.
  - Automated optimization.
- **AutoML:**
  - Google's AutoML platform provides tools for automated model design.

4. **Generative AI (Recap and Expansion):**
   - **Creating New Content:**
     - Generative AI models can create new content, such as images, text, and music.
     - This has applications in content creation, design, and entertainment.
   - **Multimodal Generation:**
     - Generating content that combines multiple modalities, such as text and images.
     - Gemini models, as previously discussed, exemplify this trend.

- Applications:
  - Personalized content generation.
  - Interactive storytelling.
  - Creative tools.

5. **Explainable AI (XAI):**
   - **Understanding Model Decisions:**
     - XAI aims to make AI models more transparent and understandable.
     - This is crucial for building trust and ensuring accountability.
   - **Techniques:**
     - Visualization tools.
     - Feature importance analysis.
     - Rule-based explanations.
   - **Benefits:**
     - Enhanced trust and transparency.
     - Improved model debugging.
     - Ethical AI development.

6. **AI for Accessibility:**
   - **Enhancing Accessibility for Users with Disabilities:**
     - AI can be used to create accessible applications for users with disabilities.

- This includes features such as voice control, image captioning, and real-time translation.
  - **Applications:**
    - Assistive technologies.
    - Accessibility tools.
    - Inclusive design.

7. **AI and Augmented Reality (AR):**
   - **Creating Immersive AR Experiences:**
     - AI can be used to create more immersive and interactive AR experiences.
     - This includes features such as object recognition, scene understanding, and real-time translation.
   - **Applications:**
     - AR navigation.
     - AR gaming.
     - AR education.

Practical Considerations:

- **Hardware Acceleration:**
  - As AI models become more complex, hardware acceleration (GPUs, NPUs) will become even more crucial.
- **Power Efficiency:**
  - Power efficiency will be a key consideration for AI on mobile and embedded devices.
- **Data Privacy:**
  - Privacy-preserving techniques, such as federated learning, will become increasingly important.
- **Ethical AI Development:**
  - Ethical considerations, such as bias and fairness, will play a critical role in AI development.

My Take:

I'm incredibly excited about the future of AI development on Android. The emerging trends and technologies we've discussed have the potential to revolutionize how we interact with technology and create truly transformative experiences.

Key Considerations:

- Stay up-to-date with the latest AI research and developments.

- Experiment with new technologies and techniques.

- Prioritize ethical AI development and user privacy.

- Consider the hardware limitations and power consumption of Android devices.

- Always refer to the most up to date Google developer documentation.

11.2 The Evolution of On-Device Generative AI

We're witnessing a paradigm shift in AI, with generative models moving from cloud-based servers to our very own devices. This evolution of on-device generative AI is opening up a new era of personalized and responsive experiences.

From Cloud to Device: A Shift in Paradigm

Traditionally, generative AI models, known for their computational intensity, have resided in the cloud. However, advancements in hardware and software are making on-device execution a reality.

Key Drivers of On-Device Generative AI:

1. **Hardware Advancements:**
   - **Powerful Mobile Processors:**
     - Modern mobile processors, especially those with dedicated AI accelerators (NPUs), are becoming increasingly powerful.
     - This enables them to handle complex generative models.
   - **Increased Memory:**
     - Mobile devices are equipped with larger amounts of RAM, allowing for the storage and processing of larger models.

2. **Model Optimization:**
   - **Quantization and Pruning (Recap):**
     - Techniques like quantization and pruning reduce model size and improve performance.
     - These optimizations are crucial for on-device execution.
   - **Efficient Architectures:**
     - Researchers are developing efficient model architectures specifically designed for mobile devices.

- MobileBERT and similar models are examples.

3. **Software Frameworks:**
    - **TensorFlow Lite:**
        - TensorFlow Lite is a key enabler of on-device AI.
        - It provides tools for optimizing and running models on mobile devices.
    - **ML Kit:**
        - Google's ML Kit offers pre-built APIs for common machine learning tasks, including some generative capabilities.

Benefits of On-Device Generative AI:

1. **Reduced Latency:**
    - On-device processing eliminates the need to send data to the cloud, resulting in faster response times.
    - This enables real-time generative experiences.
2. **Enhanced Privacy:**
    - User data remains on the device, enhancing privacy and security.

○ This is crucial for applications that handle sensitive information.

3. **Offline Functionality:**
   ○ On-device generative AI allows applications to function even without an internet connection.
   ○ This is beneficial for users in areas with limited connectivity.

4. **Personalization:**
   ○ On-device models can be fine-tuned to user preferences and data.
   ○ This enables highly personalized generative experiences.

Use Cases for On-Device Generative AI:

1. **Personalized Content Generation:**
   ○ Generating personalized stories, poems, or images based on user preferences.
   ○ This can be used in creative applications and social media.

2. **Real-Time Image and Video Editing:**
   ○ Applying generative AI techniques to edit images and videos in real-time.

- This can include style transfer, image inpainting, and video generation.

3. **Interactive Storytelling and Games:**
   - Creating interactive narratives and games that adapt to user choices.
   - This enables personalized and dynamic storytelling experiences.

4. **Personalized Assistants:**
   - Generating personalized responses and recommendations based on user context and history.
   - This can enhance the functionality of virtual assistants.

Practical Considerations:

1. **Resource Management:**
   - On-device generative AI can be resource-intensive.
   - Optimize models and code to minimize power consumption and memory usage.

2. **Model Size:**
   - Model size is a critical factor for on-device execution.

- Use techniques like quantization and pruning to reduce model size.

3. **Hardware Compatibility:**
  - Ensure that your models are compatible with the target Android devices.
  - Test your models on a variety of devices.

4. **Security:**
  - Implement security measures to protect models and user data on the device.
  - Prevent model tampering and unauthorized access.

My Take:

I'm incredibly excited about the potential of on-device generative AI. It's a game-changer that will enable us to build more responsive, personalized, and private AI experiences on Android.

Key Considerations:

- Optimize models for on-device execution.
- Consider resource management and hardware compatibility.
- Prioritize user privacy and security.

- Explore the use cases of on-device generative AI in your applications.
- Always refer to the most up to date Google developer documentation.

11.3 Resources for Continued Learning

We've covered a lot of ground, but the world of AI is ever-evolving. To truly master Android AI, continuous learning is essential. Let's explore some invaluable resources.

Your Learning Arsenal: A Curated Guide

1. **Google Developers Documentation:**
   - **TensorFlow Lite Documentation:**
     - The official TensorFlow Lite documentation is your go-to resource for on-device AI.
     - It provides comprehensive guides, tutorials, and API references.
     - TensorFlow Lite Documentation
   - **ML Kit Documentation:**
     - ML Kit offers pre-built APIs for common machine learning tasks.

- The documentation provides detailed information on using these APIs in your Android apps.
- ML Kit Documentation

- **Android AI Guides:**
  - Google provides many guides related to AI on Android, and best practices.
  - Searching the google developer website for "Android AI" will bring up many results.

- **Gemini API Documentation:**
  - As the Gemini API evolves, the google documentation will be the most accurate and up to date source of information.

2. **Google AI Blog and Research:**
   - **Google AI Blog:**
     - Stay up-to-date with the latest AI research and developments from Google.
     - The blog features articles, research papers, and announcements.
     - Google AI Blog
   - **Google AI Research:**
     - Explore Google's cutting-edge AI research.

- This can provide insights into emerging trends and technologies.
- Google AI Research

3. **Online Courses and Tutorials:**
   - **Coursera and edX:**
     - Platforms like Coursera and edX offer a wide range of AI and machine learning courses.[5]
     - These courses can provide a solid foundation in AI concepts and techniques.
   - **Fast.ai:**
     - Fast.ai offers practical and accessible deep learning courses.
     - Their courses emphasize hands-on learning and real-world applications.
   - **YouTube Channels:**
     - Many YouTube channels provide valuable AI tutorials and explanations.
     - Channels like TensorFlow and Google Developers offer relevant content.

4. **Community Forums and Stack Overflow:**
   - **Stack Overflow:**

- Stack Overflow is a great resource for troubleshooting AI-related issues.
- You can find answers to common questions and get help from experienced developers.
- **TensorFlow Forums:**
  - The TensorFlow forums provide a platform for discussing TensorFlow and TensorFlow Lite.
  - You can ask questions and share your experiences.

5. **GitHub Repositories:**
   - **TensorFlow Models Repository:**
     - The TensorFlow Models repository provides pre-trained models and example code.
     - This can be a valuable resource for learning and experimentation.
     - TensorFlow Models Repository
   - **TensorFlow Lite Examples:**
     - Google provides many TFLite example projects.

- Searching Github for "Tensorflow Lite example android" is a useful way to find these repositories.

6. **Conferences and Workshops:**

   - **Google I/O:**

     - Google I/O features sessions and workshops on the latest AI and Android technologies.
     - Attending Google I/O can provide valuable insights and networking opportunities.

   - **NeurIPS and ICML:**

     - NeurIPS and ICML are leading AI research conferences.
     - Attending these conferences can expose you to cutting-edge research.

7. **Books and Publications:**

   - **Deep Learning with Python:**

     - This book provides a practical introduction to deep learning using Keras.
     - It covers fundamental concepts and techniques.

   - **Machine Learning Engineering:**

- This book covers the engineering aspects of machine learning, including deployment and optimization.
  - **Research Papers:**
    - Reading research papers is a great way to stay up to date with the latest advancements in AI.

My Take:

I've found that continuous learning is essential for staying ahead in the rapidly evolving field of AI. By utilizing these resources, you can expand your knowledge and skills, and contribute to the exciting future of Android AI.

Key Considerations:

- Prioritize official Google documentation for the most accurate and up-to-date information.
- Explore online courses and tutorials to deepen your understanding of AI concepts.
- Engage with the AI community through forums and GitHub.

- Attend conferences and workshops to network and learn from experts.
- Read research papers and books to stay informed about cutting-edge advancements.
- Practice and experiment with the concepts that you learn.

www.ingramcontent.com/pod-product-compliance
Lightning Source LLC
LaVergne TN
LVHW081519050326
832903LV00025B/1550